REMEMBER, REMEMBER

REMEMBER, REMEMBER

A CULTURAL HISTORY OF GUY FAWKES DAY

JAMES SHARPE

HARVARD UNIVERSITY PRESS
Cambridge, Massachusetts
2005

First published in the United Kingdom in 2005
as *Remember, Remember the Fifth of November:
Guy Fawkes and the Gunpowder Plot*
Profile Books Ltd
3A Exmouth House
Pine Street
Exmouth Market
London EC1R OJH

CIP data available from the Library of Congress

ISBN 0-674-09135-0

CONTENTS

FOR GUY

Again, but for whom else could this be?

1

THE EVIL EMPIRE AND

THE ENEMY WITHIN

This is a book about remembering, commemoration, how the meaning of past events changes when cultures change. Its title comes from a rhyme which urges us to remember, a rhyme which was current by at least the early nineteenth century and has been passed on from generation to generation of Britons. As part of this process, it was taught to me by my mother when I was a child in the 1950s.

> Remember, remember, the Fifth of November,
> Gunpowder, Treason and Plot.
> I see no reason why Gunpowder Treason
> Should ever be forgot.

The rhyme has variations (it sometimes begins 'Please to remember', for example), and folklorists a century ago collected longer, more ornate versions. But these four lines are its core. The 'Gunpowder, Treason and Plot' we are asked to remember was an attempt by Roman Catholic conspirators to blow up the English Parliament, King James I of England (he was also King James VI of Scotland), other members of the royal family and leading state officials at the opening of that Parliament on 5 November 1605, an incident which, surely, deserves never to be forgotten. Indeed, in what must be the longest-established security check in history, before every state opening of the United Kingdom's Parliament the Houses of Parliament are still searched by yeoman warders in their traditional sixteenth-century uniforms.

But as time passes remembering becomes weaker and more attenuated. The remembrance of Gunpowder, Treason and Plot is no longer central in the minds of the millions of Britons who still celebrate with bonfires and fireworks every year on or around 5 November. The forgetting of the Plot's importance has been a long process. About thirty years ago it was still common to see children on the streets of English cities with effigies of the only one of those Catholic conspirators who is remembered by name, Guy Fawkes, begging 'a penny for the Guy'. My then Head of Department at the University of York, the late Gerald Aylmer, an eminent historian of seventeenth-century England, would give twopence to those urchins who could tell him who Guy Fawkes was, and (he being a generous man) a penny to those who could not. I never consulted him as to how many received twopence, but my own experience in this respect was not encouraging. Once, when asked by a child for a penny for a Guy, I refused on the grounds that I had been baptised a Catholic, and was asked what that had to do with it. Clearly this child was not equipped to remember very well, and had indeed more or less 'forgot' the nature of Gunpowder Treason.

And remembering also alters. Older British readers will remember changes in how 5 November has been celebrated over the last half-century: the decline of family bonfire nights, of numbers of children begging pennies for the Guy, the diminution of community bonfires on street-corner bombsites, the burgeoning of firework regulations. But if the way the Fifth has been celebrated over the last half-century has changed, how much more is that true of how and why it has been celebrated in the four centuries which have followed 5 November 1605. Few people, even those who know the basic outline of the history of the Plot, will be aware that between 1606 and 1859 the Fifth was remembered in an annual service of thanksgiving, in theory held in every Anglican church; or that it became a flashpoint in a number of periods of intense religious (and by extension political) strife, notably in the years around 1680 and the early 1850s; or that for much of the nineteenth century 5 November presented an annual law and order issue in many of England's towns, because it became an occasion when the rougher elements of urban society took on the new police forces and the new borough corporations who inaugurated them in an attempt to remember the Fifth of November in what they conceived as the traditional way. So this book does not simply tell the story of the Gunpowder Plot: it also tells how remembering the Fifth of November has changed over the centuries, and why and how this failed act of terrorism of four centuries ago have not been forgotten.

Remembering is helped by the dramatic circumstances of the Plot's discovery, the occasion of one of the most recognisable tableaux in English history: the tall, defiant man, bearded and long-haired, lantern in hand, dressed in a long dark cloak and a high-crowned, floppy-brimmed hat; in front of him his captors, carrying lanterns and swords, amazed and appalled by what they have found; behind him, half-hidden in the gloom of the cellar where the action is taking place, a stack of barrels filled with gunpowder. The mood is caught perfectly in a near contemporary account written by the English Jesuit Father Oswald Tesimond (also known

1. *'One of the most recognisable tableaux in English history'. The capture of Guy Fawkes as depicted in 1841 by the nineteenth-century artist and caricaturist George Cruikshank in William Harrison Ainsworth's* Guy Fawkes, or the Gunpowder Treason. *Ainsworth's book, written as it was by one of the most popular novelists of the period, was important in both symbolising and helping create a new attitude to the Gunpowder Plot. If nothing else, Cruikshank's print catches the drama of the incident.*

as Greenway). Tesimond had been involved on the fringes of the Plot, knew about it by July 1605, and was strongly (although probably erroneously) suspected by the English authorities of having advised and given spiritual comfort to the plotters. His account of the discovery of the conspiracy, translated from his original Italian, runs as follows:

Parliament was due to begin on Tuesday, 5 November. On the Monday night preceding, Sir Thomas Knyvett, a gentleman of the King's household, was sent to search the lower rooms and cellars beneath the actual chamber where Parliament met. He was to make his search as if he were concerned with other matters. But notice that at the entrance of the outer chambers he meets a man fully dressed, booted and spurred! Since it was already past midnight, this seemed to him rather strange. Knyvett therefore had him seized by some of his officials. Next he went to the cellar and asked for the keys. He found that the man they had already arrested had them. They made him open the cellar, and immediately began to move the bundles of wood. Their first find was a small barrel of gunpowder, and after that a number of barrels arranged in order to the number of thirty-six, large and small. Nearby was a dark lantern with the candle lit inside. From this they immediately concluded what it was. They had the man searched whom they had just seized. Three fuses, or matches, were found on him, one shorter than the others, and three tubes through which to pass them. These would serve to ignite the powder on the following morning.

The man taken was Guy Fawkes, one of a group of malcontent Roman Catholic conspirators. He was in a 'cellar' (in fact a ground-floor storeroom) under the Palace of Westminster because he had the responsibility of igniting those thirty-six barrels of gunpowder and blowing sky-high King James, his wife Anne, his sons Henry and Charles, and the members of the House of Lords and the House of Commons.

Guy Fawkes has become one of that select body of characters from English history who are instantly recognisable, and is also remembered, in an old joke, as the only man ever to enter Parliament with honest intentions. His effigy has been burnt annually on thousands of bonfires, and the Plot that was uncovered so dramatically in 1605 is commemorated on every Fifth of November. But now, four centuries later, the annual ritual is very distant from the Plot's original resonances, and it is all too easy to forget its impact on contemporaries, and on the generations which immediately followed. Nearly a century and a half after the Plot, on 5 November 1745, Samuel Baker was preaching at York in the face of the latest Catholic threat against the Protestant English way of life, launched by Charles Edward Stuart and his invading army of Scottish Highlanders. In the course of his sermon, Baker conjured up a vivid impression of what would have happened if Fawkes had succeeded in his mission:

> Imagine the fatal blow given; the severed heads, the mangled limbs, the torn bodies tossed and scattered in the air; mixed with a shower of blood, spouting from their burst and rented veins. Hear the dismal crack bring out the affrighted multitude, see them with sorrow and amazement gazing at the confounding, dreadful ruin: view the distressed mother, the tender wife, pale and trembling, seeking for the sad remains of son and husband; tired with the horrid, and fruitless search,

returning with wringing hands and bloated eyes, and rending the skies with doleful exclamations, and cries for vengeance!

'By gloomy bigotry was this contrived,' Baker reminded his audience, 'and relentless popery.'

Samuel Baker was clearly aiming for maximum effect, but a more scientific modern calculation of what would have happened had Guy Fawkes ignited the powder is sobering enough. In 2003 the Institute of Physics in London asked scientists at the University of Aberystwyth's Centre for Explosion Studies to estimate the probable effects of detonating thirty-six barrels of gunpowder under the old House of Lords. The exercise, as the scientists made clear, had to be an approximate one. Translating thirty-six barrels of gunpowder into an exact weight is difficult, as is making any definite comparison between seventeenth-century gunpowder and modern explosives. The Aberystwyth team estimated that the amount of explosives would be about 5,000lb, and decided, admittedly constructing a worst-case scenario, to assume that the gunpowder used by the plotters would have a force equivalent to that of TNT. On this basis, they calculated that Fawkes, if successful in his mission, would have caused structural damage within a radius of 500 yards. All buildings within forty yards would have been destroyed, roofs and walls within a 100-yard radius would have collapsed, and even at 900 yards some windows would have been broken. The Palace of Westminster, Westminster Hall, Westminster Abbey and the surrounding streets would have been obliterated. Perhaps the scenario would not have been so very different from that imagined by our eighteenth-century preacher. At the very least, it would have been a daring and major terrorist attack, both in terms of the damage it inflicted and in its propaganda value.

Who, in the early twenty-first century, could fail to be reminded of 11 September 2001, of that unforgettable image of the airliners slicing into the twin towers, of their collapse, of the dead and the injured, and of the dust-covered survivors walking through the rubble? The conflicting reactions to the tragic events of 9/11 are surely relevant too. As always, one person's terrorist can be another's freedom fighter, another's holy martyr in a righteous cause. Perhaps the story of the Gunpowder Plot is one of those moments of history which might make us understand our current predicaments a little better, and perhaps warn us how not to make those predicaments worse.

THE CATHOLIC THREAT

What made the Catholic attempt to destroy the King, the royal family, the Commons and the Lords all the more credible was that, to English Protestants of 1605, that was exactly the sort of thing Catholics *did*. English Protestant identity had been constructed against a background of tales of popish oppressions and popish atrocities. Indeed, the very birth of the Church of England as it existed in 1605 was inseparable from what quickly became thought of as Catholic tyranny. In 1553 the young Edward VI, a keen supporter of advanced Protestantism, had died, and the throne had passed to his elder sister Mary Tudor. The new Queen was initially popular, but this popularity waned after she married the King of Spain, Philip II, and set about a programme of re-Catholicization in England. Reviving the old religion need not have been that difficult, as the bulk of the

2. *Protestant identity in Elizabethan England was constructed partly around an unfolding history of Catholic atrocity. Here, in an illustration from John Foxe's* Acts and Monuments *(known popularly as* The Book of Martyrs*), preparations are being made to burn seven Protestants at Smithfield, London, during the reign of Mary Tudor.*

population was probably Catholic or willing to be reconciled to Catholicism. But Mary and her advisers sought to promote the return to the old faith by burning heretics, and 237 men and fifty-two women were consigned to the flames between February 1555 and the Queen's death in November 1558. A few of these were highly placed clerics, but most of them were relatively lowly men and women, farmers, craftsmen and the like: several hundred richer Protestants had gone into exile. Had Mary lived longer, her policies might well eventually have proved successful. But her early death was followed by the arrival of a Protestant regime with her younger sister Elizabeth at its head, and the history of Mary's reign became enshrined in an avidly Protestant interpretation. In 1563 the first English edition of John Foxe's *Acts and Monuments*, which was to become better known as

The Book of Martyrs, was published. This was a massively important work, establishing a history that sought to demonstrate the existence of a Church of England long before the Reformation, and stressed the importance of divine providence in preserving that Church against Romanist corruptions. But the most vivid message for most of its readers was the heroic story of Protestant resistance to Catholic oppression during Mary's reign. Over the next two centuries this constantly reprinted work was to become one of the most read books in the English language.

The next propaganda disaster for English Catholicism was provided not by a monarch, but by a Pope, Pius V. Mary Queen of Scots, a Catholic ruler with a reasonable claim to the English throne, arrived in England as an exile in 1568, and her subsequent presence there was to constitute a source of continual political instability. Mary made no secret of her belief that she could set up a monarchy in England with the support of the northern English nobility; many of these were still attached to Catholicism, and were more generally becoming alienated from a central government which, as they saw it, was gradually easing them out of power. Two of the most significant northern nobles, Charles Neville, Earl of Westmoreland, and Thomas Percy, Earl of Northumberland, had recently re-converted to Catholicism. Westmoreland was brother-in-law to Thomas Howard, Duke of Norfolk, the most powerful noble in the land, a closet Catholic who was planning to marry Mary Queen of Scots and head a Catholic regime in England. Plots and rumours of plots proliferated, and when Northumberland and Westmoreland were ordered to go to London and explain their conduct in 1569, they raised a rebellion centred on County Durham. The Northern Rising of 1569 was easily suppressed once the government recovered its nerve and sent an army north: a few hundred of the rebels were executed, 300 villages were burnt, fifty northern castles were razed. Westmoreland went into exile in the Netherlands and Northumberland in Scotland (he was executed at York in 1572 after the Scots sent him back to Elizabeth in return for £2,000). All of this was bad enough for the Catholic cause in England; but the rising left long-term repercussions following the decision by Pope Pius V in February 1570 to issue his papal bull *Regnans in Excelsis* ('ruling from on high' – a reference to God). This excommunicated Elizabeth, declared her to be no true monarch, and in effect gave her subjects the right to depose her. From then on any English Catholic could be regarded as a potential traitor, and the mighty forces of international Catholicism could be portrayed as having a fifth column of potential traitors, rebels and regicides in England. An enemy within had been created.

To make matters worse, in the eyes of Elizabeth's regime, from the early 1570s this fifth column had its resolve strengthened by help from abroad. In the first decade of Elizabeth's reign about 100 Catholic academics and clergy, most of them from Oxford, had left an England which was becoming daily more Protestant and had settled in Catholic areas of the continent. One such was William Allen, formerly head of an Oxford college and a scholar of some repute, who in 1568 founded a college for the ordination of English priests at Douai in the Habsburg Netherlands. Allen, a conservative academic, had not envisaged his college as a training centre for missionary priests who would dedicate their lives to keeping the Catholic faith alive in England. But many of his students did, and in 1574 three of them crossed the Channel. By the end of Elizabeth's reign about 450 foreign-trained English Catholic priests had entered the country, from Douai, from the English college in Rome (another training centre for priests), formally settled in 1579, and from similar English colleges in Spain, at Valladolid and Seville. Just over 130 of them were executed, along with sixty or so lay people who had helped or sheltered them. They died, the English government insisted, for treason rather than for their religious beliefs. The courage of these priests, and of those succouring them, was outstanding, and stories of their sufferings both bolstered English Catholic consciousness and dismayed English officialdom. Even worse from the English Protestant point of view was the ever-increasing Jesuit input into the English mission. The Society of Jesus, founded in 1540, rapidly established itself as a vital agency in the Catholic Counter-Reformation. Jesuits were well trained, were skilled disputants, and were part of a hierarchical, disciplined, tightly controlled and centralised organisation. Any penetration of England by Catholic priests was bad enough: but the knowledge that the spirits of English Catholics were being strengthened by these stormtroopers of the Counter-Reformation was a source of constant worry to the English government, and provoked vicious comment from that government's propagandists.

In 1588 English Protestants were also confronted by an external threat of massive proportions in the shape of the Spanish Armada. Philip II had long, and with considerable justification, been irritated by the activities of English adventurers (the Spanish called them pirates) in the Caribbean, while from 1585 English military support for Philip's rebellious Dutch subjects gave the Spanish monarch a more serious, and certainly more local, cause for concern. He therefore gathered a fleet of about 125 ships carrying nearly 19,000 soldiers. This Armada was to sail into the Channel, and not only to land the troops it carried in England but also to ferry over a proportion of Philip's Army of Flanders, which was probably the most effective fighting force in Europe. But in the event, after inconclusive running battles in the Channel, the Armada was panicked into breaking formation by English fire ships off Calais, given a severe drubbing at Gravelines, and then dispersed by bad weather. This bad weather, to English propagandists, was a sign of a divine intervention as powerful as that which had saved the English from Mary Tudor. But these same propagandists were not slow to point out what the consequences of a successful Spanish invasion might have been. As the hack writer Thomas Deloney put it, the Spanish would come:

> To kill and murder man and wife as malice doth
> arise;
> and to deflower our virgins in our sight;
> and in the cradel cruelly the tender babe to smite.

In another ballad Deloney informed his readers that among the vessels sailing with the Armada was a boat laden with different types of whips, with which the Spaniards were planning to lash the English back into Catholicism. Thus the Catholic threat now included Philip II and the might of what was, in the late sixteenth century, the major European super-power, Catholic Spain. And, with scant regard for accuracy, English propagandists were to make much of supposed papal involvement in the Armada, thus adding another potent ingredient to the mix.

Warnings of impending Spanish atrocities were rendered all the more powerful by a knowledge of what Catholics,

Spaniards and others, had accomplished abroad. In Elizabeth's reign English Protestants could see two of their country's closest neighbours being racked by wars of religion. In France a mix of weak monarchs, the political ambitions of the high nobility and religious strife had, from 1562, created a situation of endemic and occasionally bitter warfare between Catholics and the Huguenots, as French Protestants were known. In 1570 the third bout of conflict had ended, and the resultant peace settlement had granted a limited toleration to the Huguenots and marked a setback for the immensely powerful and rabidly Catholic Guise family. The situation was clearly uneasy, and in particular the Guises plotted revenge against Coligny, the Huguenot leader. In August 1572 most of the French nobility were gathered in Paris, where a wedding was taking place between another Huguenot notable, Henri of Navarre, and Marguerite de Valois, sister-in-law of the French monarch, a marriage intended to symbolise the end of religious conflict and help ensure lasting religious peace in France. It failed miserably in these objectives. On 22 August, four days after the nuptials, Coligny was shot at and wounded from the window of a nearby house as he walked in the street. On 24 August, St Bartholomew's Day, he was murdered in his sickbed by the Duke of Guise and other Catholic noblemen, and the population of Paris rose to carry out what appears to have been a spontaneous massacre of Huguenots. At least 2,000 Protestants, and maybe twice that number, were massacred in the city, while similar anti-Huguenot violence in provincial towns may have brought the total up to 10,000 nationally. The killings, remembered among English Protestants as the St Bartholomew's Day Massacre, neither exterminated the Huguenots nor ended the French Wars of Religion. What they did was give Protestantism in Europe as a whole and in England in particular a terrifying vision of what Catholics might do if given a chance.

Although the Dutch Revolt was to produce no single atrocity as spectacular as the St Bartholomew's Day Massacre, it certainly gave Protestants enough cause for concern. The revolt had begun in the early 1560s primarily as a movement of a disgruntled high nobility against a regime with which they had fallen out of sympathy, but it gradually assumed, both in the Low Countries and in the eyes of Europe as a whole, the character of a religious war, with brave Protestant rebels defying, and rather against the odds defeating, the Catholic superpower which oppressed them. This interpretation was certainly spread by an anonymous account of the struggle, published in English in 1583 as *A Tragicall Historie of the Warres in the Low Countries*, which provided the English reader with yet more accounts of oppressions and atrocities carried out by Catholic priests and Philip II's soldiers. And, in all conscience, some of these atrocities were real enough. In 1567 the Duke of Alva was sent to the Netherlands to crush the revolt by military means. He adopted deliberate terror as a technique for bringing Philip II's errant subjects under control, as he set about a steady process of besieging and conquering rebel towns. The worst incident came in December 1572. After lesser atrocities at the newly conquered towns of Mechlin and Zutphen, Alva ordered the killing of every man, woman and child in the next town he took, Naarden. Coming only a few months after the St Bartholomew's Day Massacre, Naarden provided Protestants with another powerful story of atrocity, and the Duke of Alva joined the growing list of Catholic bogeymen. The Spanish reconquest of the Netherlands was frustrated in

1575, when the Spanish treasury went bankrupt. The pay of the Army of Flanders fell many months into arrears, and isolated and spontaneous acts of rapine rapidly replaced any calculated campaign of terror. The most spectacular of these came in 1576, when Spanish troops devastated Antwerp, the richest city in the Netherlands. For several days the troops ran riot, raping, killing and pillaging. Recent research suggests that only a few hundred of Antwerp's citizens, most of them probably Catholic, were killed. But Protestant commentators were soon confidently quoting a total of 17,000, while English readers were treated to an account of the affair pointedly entitled *A Larum for London or the Siedge of Antwerpe*. The 'Spanish Fury' at Antwerp thus joined the list of Catholic atrocities, while, a few years later, tales of massacres, oppressions and forced conversions by Spaniards and Catholic priests gained a wider geographical basis with the publication of *The Spanish Colonie, or Brief Chronicle of the Actes and Gestes of the Spaniards in the West Indies*, a translation of a critique of the brutal treatment of the native peoples in the Spanish Americas originally published by Bartolomé de Las Casas in 1551. The English terror of what might have happened had the Armada been successful was profoundly deepened by this 'Black Legend' of Spain's brutality against its subjects in both Europe and the Americas.

As well as these atrocities and oppressions – and very pertinently for the Gunpowder Plot – Catholics had also assassinated some very highly placed individuals. Perhaps the most relevant of these, apart from Coligny in August 1572, was William the Silent, Count of Nassau and Prince of Orange, leader of the Dutch rebels. William had survived a number of assassination attempts, some carried out with Spanish backing, but on 10 July 1584 he was finally shot dead in his palace at Delft. His killer was a young Burgundian, Balthazar Gérard, an ardent Catholic who had vowed to kill the arch-heretic. In 1589 Henri III, King of France, was to suffer a similar fate. By this date the French Wars of Religion had become a three-cornered contest, between the monarchy and its moderate Catholic supporters, the Huguenots and the Catholic League, a hardline Catholic organisation headed by the Guise family and backed by Spain and the papacy. In May 1588 the power of the League was demonstrated when the population of Paris, a Catholic hotbed, denied access to the city to Henri and his troops. At the end of 1588 Henri III gained his revenge when both the Duke of Guise and his brother the Cardinal of Guise were murdered by the King's bodyguard, and a number of leading League nobles imprisoned. But these actions prompted an immediate reaction in Paris, with the Sorbonne absolving all Frenchmen from their oath of allegiance to Henri in much the same way that Pius V had absolved Elizabeth's subjects from loyalty to their monarch. A young friar called Jacques Clement, influenced by the frenzied atmosphere in Paris, on 1 August 1589 gained access to the King under a pretence and fatally stabbed him. So a King of France, himself a Catholic, was added to the victims of hardline Catholicism.

Famously, Ronald Reagan described the Soviet Union and its satellite states as an 'Evil Empire'. This label would have been perfectly understandable to English public opinion had it been applied to Catholicism in the years around 1600. Here was a religious system which was capable of dreadful atrocities, in France, in the Low Countries, in the Indies, and, with the Marian burnings, in England. At its centre sat the Pope, perceived as a universal spider whose aim was no less than world domination, and who was happy to depose monarchs and encourage their subjects to rise against them to achieve it. Apart from these encouragements to rebellion and deposition, Catholics were capable of assassinating highly-placed opponents to further their ends. They had, in the form of Spain's army and ships, the resources of the most powerful superpower in Europe at their disposal, and, more particularly, in the form of the Army of Flanders, soldiers with a proven track record both of military prowess and anti-Protestant atrocity. And, in the Jesuits, the Pope and the King of Spain possessed a body of dedicated and fearless ideological agents, anxious to spread the Catholic faith across the world, skilled in controversy, alert to the effectiveness of controlling minds through a superb educational system, willing to undergo privation and death in the furtherance of their cause. This, in the English Protestant imagination, was an Evil Empire indeed: powerful, ruthless, willing to inflict widespread death and suffering in its unceasing quest for dominance. God had intervened, and saved the English from Catholicism, in 1558 and 1588, but there was no guarantee that he would do so again. Vigilance against the Catholic threat was therefore vital, not least when England's native Catholic population was under consideration.

ENGLISH CATHOLICISM

Protestant vigilance against England's Catholics was enshrined in a powerful body of legislation. In 1559 the Act of Supremacy and the Act of Uniformity between them made the denial of royal supremacy over the Church illegal, together with celebration of the Mass and other aspects of Catholicism, while imposing a fine of a shilling a week on people absenting themselves from the legally prescribed services of the Church of England. These were known as recusants, a word which came to be applied particularly to Roman Catholic absentees. During the parliamentary session of 1562-3 penalties were imposed for upholding the authority of the Pope, while the Oath of Supremacy was imposed as a test of religious loyalty over a wider range of laymen and clergy. These laws were quickly perceived to be ineffective, and in 1575 the Privy Council, after summoning leading Catholic gentlemen to London, imposed a number of restrictions on the civil liberties of prominent Catholics and called for a national census of recusants. Further legal measures came in 1581, with, *inter alia*, the fine for recusancy upped to £20 if four successive Sunday services were missed, while in 1583 special recusancy commissioners, with broad powers to investigate suspected Catholics, were created. In 1579, in an effort to weed out closet Catholics, the obligation to swear the Oath of Supremacy was extended to a wide range of officials and professionals, including schoolmasters, lawyers and justices of the peace. The practice of evading fines through various legal ruses was addressed by further legislation of 1586, which allowed the government to seize a recusant's goods and two-thirds of his lands until he had paid the fine he was attempting to evade, conformed, or died. In 1593 another Act required Catholics to stay within five miles of their homes, with banishment as the punishment for infringements of this legislation. On a higher political level, an Act of 1571, 'Against the bringing in and putting in execution for bulls and other instruments from the see of Rome', obviously a reaction to *Regnans in Excelsis*, made it high treason to import, publish or publicise any official documents from Rome. And in 1585 yet further legislation, among other things, made it high treason to be a

Catholic priest, and declared those aiding such priests to be guilty variously of felony or misprision of treason. The legal framework thus provided a means for fining the generality of Catholics into conformity and executing Catholic priests or Catholic activists as traitors.

Implementing these laws was far from straightforward. In the early years of Elizabeth's reign many justices of the peace or members of urban elites were of a broadly Catholic persuasion, or at least conservative in religion, and hence unlikely to pursue recusants too vigorously. Throughout the reign, many justices, themselves recruited from the gentry, were unwilling to persecute too heavily those Catholics in their vicinity who were themselves gentlemen: social solidarity cut across religious loyalties. The reporting of recusants under the 1559 legislation, whose shilling recusancy fine became increasingly vital in the persecution of poorer Catholics, depended on local churchwardens, whose efficiency could not always be relied upon, especially when it meant reporting neighbours or kinsfolk, or important people within the parish whom it might be inadvisable to cross. And, of course, there were probably people of all social ranks who simply found persecution in matters of religion repugnant. Few even of those willing to persecute reached the level of commitment of the Lincolnshire gentleman Richard Topcliffe, according to the Jesuit John Gerard 'the cruellest tyrant of all England ... a man most infamous and hateful to all the realm for his bloody and butcherly mind'. Topcliffe, apparently with official permission, kept a private rack in his house upon which he tortured Catholics, his treatment of the Jesuit Robert Southwell according to tradition generating so much criticism that he had to be imprisoned briefly for exceeding his warrant. Generally, however, the use of special officers known as poursuivants to hunt recusants was felt by local authorities to cut across known and accepted legal and administrative procedures, while informers were usually not very popular, even with justices. Moreover, the familiarity with the legal system and family connections of gentry Catholics frequently allowed them, even after the 1586 Act, to evade the worst of the financial penalties laid upon them.

These problems, from the government's point of view, were compounded by the presence of 'church papists', people who remained Catholic at heart but who went through the formalities of attending Church of England services frequently enough to keep them out of trouble, typically refusing to take communion, and possibly observing their own faith in private. Such people were the despair both of the authorities, in their desire to identify and penalise Catholics, and, from the mid-1570s, of those Catholic missionary priests who came to England and who wished for a higher level of overt commitment from their flock. The presence of these occasional conformists greatly complicated an issue which was of considerable concern to the Elizabethan authorities and has attracted the attention of later historians: namely, exactly how many Catholics there were in England. Nationally, the best estimates seem to suggest that in 1603 they formed less than 1 per cent of the population, maybe 40,000 people. But such estimates conceal two important features of English Catholicism: its geographical distribution and its class composition. Catholics could, of course, exist everywhere: even in 'Puritan' Essex the Petre family survived for generation after generation in the old faith. But some areas were perceived as being especially prone to popery. Lancashire regularly scored as the most Catholic county of all, with 6-7 per cent of its population recusant or non-communicant in 1603. Yorkshire was also regarded as a county with numerous papists, as were the Welsh border counties and the southern counties of Sussex and Hampshire. Moreover, Catholicism was increasingly turning into a religion headed by the gentry. This meant, perhaps, that it was cut off from its popular roots. But as long as most local justices of the peace were unwilling to extirpate their social equals as a necessary concomitant of eradicating popery, this gentry leadership was vital in preserving the old faith.

For maybe the first decade of Elizabeth's reign, certainly up to the papal bull of 1570, being an occasional conformist was a relatively easy option for an English Catholic. After that, it became less so. Obviously, the bull, with its implication that all Catholics were potential rebels, made the authorities more jumpy about this 'enemy within'. Moreover, the proponents of Protestantism in England were growing more confident. Every year the Elizabethan Settlement survived, it grew more firmly established in the hearts and minds of English men and women; and one aspect of its growing sense of authority was that it felt increasingly able to take on its opponents, and draw the dividing lines between the old faith and the new more distinctly and police those lines more rigorously. On the other side, the seminary priests who were arriving in England from the mid-1570s onwards were equally anxious to establish these dividing lines in hopes of producing an active and informed Catholicism. All this had political overtones. Even the most apolitical of Catholics had sooner or later to confront the issue of how his or her religious community stood in relation to the wider political entity of England, the symbol of whose unity was the monarchy. But despite being pressured by both their monarch's government and their priests to stand up and be counted, many Catholics retained what was essentially a passive position, maintaining (in defiance of most contemporary political theorists) that their religion was their own business, and not the Queen's.

What made such a position easier, and indeed what made the survival of Catholicism possible, was its transformation into a household, and especially a gentry household, religion. On one level, this trait was not unique to Catholicism: Protestant writers, too, emphasised the importance of the godly household as one of the essential building blocks of society. But for England's Catholics, unlike her Protestants, there was no opportunity for public worship. The recusant house became the place where Mass was celebrated, communion taken, where baptisms and marriages took place, where holy-days were observed, where children were instructed in the faith. This dependence on the gentry household gave English Catholicism a source of strength. The Midland recusant nobleman Lord Vaux, in trouble in 1581, along with his family and servants, for not attending his parish church at Harrowden, 'did claim his house to be a parish by itself'. This attitude, with its implicit assumption of gentry particularism, was probably one which many of Vaux's non-Catholic social equals could sympathise with. This integration of religion into the household also helped bind social ties, especially if tenants and Catholic neighbours were involved. And, as a final great advantage, it gave the Catholic householder considerable control over Catholic priests, whose ability to function, indeed whose very survival, depended on men like Vaux. For whatever Catholic gentry and noblemen may have wanted, a religious set-up in which their interests were subordinate to those of the clergy

3. *By the end of Elizabeth's reign, English Catholics had their martyrs too. Here, in an illustration from Richard Verstegan's* Theatrum Crudelitatum Haereticorum nostri Temporis, *the pressing to death of Margaret Clitherow at York in 1586 is depicted: Guy Fawkes, brought up in York, was converting to Catholicism at roughly this point. Verstegan was the son of Low Countries parents who settled in England, adopting the name of Rowlands, but he returned to the Low Countries and resumed the family name when England finally turned to Protestantism. His great work on Protestant atrocities against Catholics was frequently published after its first appearance in 1583 in numerous Latin and French editions.*

was not on the agenda, however much individual priests may have been respected and protected.

Women too, as all modern writers on the subject are agreed, were important to the survival of Catholicism. Explaining why is difficult. There may be something in the comment of John Bossy, one of the major historians of the English Catholic community, that 'the average woman of the upper classes might reasonably feel that the Reformation had not been designed with her in mind'. More prosaically, a family wishing to maintain its Catholicism might adopt a strategy whereby the husband remained outwardly conformist while the wife, less likely to incur the full rigour of the law, would maintain an overt attachment to Catholicism. Under English Common Law (to which the persecution of recusants had effectively been passed in 1581) a married woman was a *feme covert*, not a person with a legal existence. Prosecuting such people for breaches of the law posed obvious technical and conceptual problems, while attempts to shift the recusancy fines that should have been imposed on such women on to their husbands obviously proved unpopular. But for whatever reason, gentry women remained a mainstay of English Catholicism, while their central role in bringing up children helped ensure that the faith would be passed on to the next generation. Many of these women showed great courage and extreme devotion: indeed, the most celebrated lay Catholic martyr of the Elizabethan period was a woman, Margaret Clitherow [or Clitheroe] of York. In 1571 Margaret, herself from an established background in the city, married a prosperous butcher, John Clitherow. Her husband was a Protestant, but his brother William was a Catholic priest, and it was probably under his influence that Margaret entered the faith, becoming a Catholic in 1574. From that date until 1586 she frequently fell foul of the authorities, and was imprisoned on several occasions. Finally, in 1586 she was indicted for sheltering and aiding Jesuit and seminary priests, and, after refusing to plead, was subjected to the *peine forte et dure* and pressed to death in York Castle. In a striking demonstration of loyalty to their mother's religion, her son Henry and stepson William both became priests, while her daughter Anne became a nun in a convent at Louvain.

As Clitherow's fate demonstrates, being a Roman Catholic in late Elizabethan England might incur tragic consequences, and it is hardly surprising that a Catholic historian, Hugh Aveling, should label the years 1583 to 1603 as 'The Heroic Years of Catholic Recusancy'. If Mary Tudor, via John Foxe, was to provide English Protestants with a tradition of oppression and martyrdom, her successor was to do much the same for English Catholics. For many Catholics, the experience of living through those two decades must have been comparable to that of members of resistance movements in Nazi-occupied Europe: a willingness to die for a cause which must have seemed hopeless, existing in a world of uncertainty and danger, a world where it was difficult to gauge whom to trust. Not all, perhaps only a few, Catholics were committed on this level. But for all of them there was the constant problem of keeping their faith alive, maintaining contacts both nationally and internationally, helping their co-religionists, and, above all, harbouring priests and helping sustain those networks which allowed priests to operate. Many of these priests were from gentry background, and all of them were well educated, so it was relatively easy for them to pass themselves off as gentlemen and thus evade suspicion. But all of them were dependent, at one time or another, on the goodwill of lay people, and many of them were to be forced to take refuge in the priest-holes, those hiding places which existed in the manor houses of the Catholic gentry and which are regularly shown to modern tourists. For both the priests and those who sheltered them, the consequences of being found could be a terrible death.

Yet even in the face of this persecution it seems that most of England's Catholics remained loyal to their monarch and wanted nothing more than to be allowed to practise their faith unmolested. Indeed, despite the recusancy laws and the rhetoric of government propaganda, some Catholics prospered under Elizabeth I. Perhaps a uniquely successful example was Anthony Browne, first Viscount Montague, the son of one of Henry VIII's courtiers and himself a man who had prospered under Mary Tudor. Montague did not change his religion after Elizabeth came to the throne, but nevertheless was entrusted with a number of offices by the Queen, and was to demonstrate his loyalty by turning up with 200 horsemen at Tilbury in 1588 when Elizabeth was amassing forces to confront the Armada. Montague's overt loyalty, aided by his ability to avoid any politically suspect entanglements, ensured not only his own family's good fortunes but also those of the Catholics around his estates in Sussex. Perhaps more remarkable was Sir Thomas Tresham, an eminent and wealthy Northamptonshire Catholic. Tresham was heavily and repeatedly fined, and on several occasions imprisoned, for his faith, and built, on the family estate at Rushton, the famous 'Triangular Lodge', a building resembling nothing so much as a folly but which was, in fact, more or less a shrine to his sufferings and to the Roman Catholic faith. Yet Tresham was unrelenting in his support for the Elizabethan regime. In particular, in 1585 he was one of the leaders of a body of Catholic noblemen and gentry who, in the face of yet more severe legislation, presented a petition to the Queen assuring her of their loyalty and begging for a lessening of the severity of persecution. The loyalty was expressed largely in traditional and possibly outdated terms, but it also disassociated the petitioners from plots against the Queen, regicide, and papal pretensions to depose monarchs. Tresham's correspondence demonstrates that he held such views throughout his life, while in March 1603 it was he who loyally proclaimed the accession of James I to the populace of Northampton. This caused grumblings among the local Puritans, who were dismayed to see so notorious a recusant proclaiming the arrival on the throne of a Protestant monarch.

The continuation of loyalty among the English Catholic laity was mirrored to some extent by some fundamental splits among the English Catholic clergy which were opening up in the final years of Elizabeth's reign. Although there were rarely more than five Jesuit priests active in England at any one time in the late sixteenth century, they had a disproportionate impact on the English mission, a fact which left at least some of the English secular clergy (i.e. those not members of a religious order, such as the Society of Jesus) discontented. In 1595 any underlying resentments came very much to a head with 'stirs' in what was basically an internment camp for Catholic priests at Wisbech Castle in Norfolk. As so often, a clash over principles was inextricably enmeshed with a clash over personalities. One of the imprisoned priests, William Weston, formerly Superior of the Jesuits in England, felt that the religious and moral regime at Wisbech was too lax, and clashed on this with Christopher Bagshaw, a secular priest possibly less pious than Weston but apparently more contentious. The problems at Wisbech were paralleled by a controversy in the years 1594–7 over the degree of Jesuit control over the English college at Rome. Finally, matters came to a head with the appointment of George Blackwell as Archpriest over the English secular clergy in March 1598. Blackwell was a known friend of the Jesuits, and was keen to work with them, a position which many English secular clergy were willing to adopt but to which a few were violently hostile. These appealed to the

Pope against developments in England (hence earning themselves the title 'Appellants') only to have their criticisms
rejected, a situation which encouraged Blackwell to censure
them for schism. In the resulting controversy the Appellants
were able to voice anti-Jesuit sentiments as violent as any
put forward by Elizabethan Protestant propagandists, and,
in fact opened a split among Catholics which the government was anxious to attempt to exploit. Differences over
Church organisation, a matter of pressing importance for
English Catholic clergy, lay at the base of these disputes: but
a show of willingness by the Appellants to take a more loyal-
ist line towards Elizabeth was also an important factor.

Thus the reality of Catholicism in England around 1600
was very different from the image conjured up in government propaganda and contemporary Protestant myth. Yes,
there were some Catholics who envisaged the overthrow of
Elizabeth I and were willing to work with foreign powers,
notably Spain, to achieve that aim. But most Catholics did
not envisage rising against the government, were unlikely
to turn to Spanish support, rejected the papacy's claims
to intervene in secular affairs, and were anxious to keep
Catholic priests as firmly under control as possible, while
those very priests were, by the time of Elizabeth's death in
1603, seriously divided among themselves. Most Catholics,
faced with renewed prosecution, would simply have gritted
their teeth and borne it. But for a few Catholics that reaction no longer seemed adequate. Among them was a young
Warwickshire gentleman named Robert Catesby.

ROBERT CATESBY AND HIS CIRCLE

The Catesby family was long-established and wealthy, with

Robert's father, Sir William Catesby, owning not only the family seat at Lapworth in Warwickshire, but also other lands in Northamptonshire. But this favourable position was prejudiced by Sir William's attachment to the Catholic faith, for which he suffered fines and imprisonment. Like many of the more substantial Catholic families of the period, the Catesbys were related by marriage to a wide network of recusant gentry. Most importantly, Sir William, through his wife Anne Throckmorton of Coughton in Warwickshire, was connected with the important Throckmorton family and, through them, with another leading recusant clan, the Vaux family. This extensive cousinage was of central importance to the history of the Gunpowder Plot.

Robert (or as he was sometimes called in contemporary accounts, 'Robin') Catesby was born, so it is believed, at Lapworth in 1573. He may have spent some time at the English seminary at Douai, and he certainly studied at Oxford for a short period, at Gloucester Hall (now Worcester College), regarded at the time as a nest of Roman Catholics. But in 1593 he married Catherine Leigh, daughter of yet another Warwickshire gentry family, but in this case a Protestant. His wife's family was a wealthy one (she brought a dowry of £2,000), and the two settled on land Robert had inherited from his grandfather, apparently living happily, and having two sons, one of whom died in infancy. His wife's Protestantism protected Robert from the worst rigours of the recusancy laws (his surviving son, also named Robert, had been baptised as a Protestant), and there is every indication that he was happy to accept the role of a church papist, his position being further enhanced when he inherited his father's fortune in 1598. But this year was also to see the death of his wife, and it seems that it was this tragic loss which turned him back to the Catholic Church. From that point Catesby was noted for his total devotion to the faith of his ancestors.

As everybody who has studied the Gunpowder Plot rapidly comes to realise, it was Catesby, who has largely been forgotten, rather than Guy Fawkes, whom we all remember, who was the prime force that set in motion the train of events which was to unfold on 5 November 1605: to one of the plot's most recent historians, Antonia Fraser, Catesby was simply 'the prince of darkness at the centre of the Gunpowder Plot'. A contemporary description, by the Jesuit priest Oswald Tesimond, depicts him in attractive terms:

> Physically, Catesby was more than ordinarily well-proportioned, some six feet tall, of good carriage and handsome countenance. He was grave in manner, but attractively so. He was also considered one of the most dashing and courageous horsemen in the county. Generous and affable, he was for that reason much loved by everyone.

Catesby did seem to have a capacity to inspire people, and to persuade them to accept his point of view. As the author of his entry in the first, Victorian, edition of the *Dictionary of National Biography* put it, 'he is said to have exercised a magical influence upon all who mixed with him.'

As we have noted, Catesby possessed a network of Catholic kin, and a number of his relatives are important in our story. Among them were the brothers Robert and Thomas Winter [or Wintour] of Huddington Court, Worcestershire (Robert was born in 1568, Thomas in 1571), whose sister, Dorothy, was married to another recusant gentleman, John

Grant. Thomas, who was a particular friend of Catesby, was described by Tesimond as an intelligent young man who had studied philosophy, and who was noted for his wisdom. Physically, he was 'short of stature, but agile enough, well-built and of good carriage. His face was round but handsome, with eyes that were wide awake and vivacious. He was a man of pleasing manners.' Another of Catesby's cousins was Francis Tresham, heir to the redoubtable Sir Thomas.

Thus Catesby was connected by kinship to a wide network of recusant families. His was not, of course, the only such network, and there is another which is of great relevance to our story. The central characters here were John and Christopher Wright, young gentlemen of the same generation as the Winters and Francis Tresham (John was born in 1568 and Christopher in 1570), burly young men who liked action and were noted for their swordsmanship, but who were also devout Catholics. According to Tesimond (and here as elsewhere we have to depend on the evidence of a biased source), John Wright 'had a good physique and sound constitution', and was a man who in his youth had been renowned for his courage, 'and was considered the best swordsman of his day'. He was tall, with pleasing features, although he was 'somewhat taciturn in manner, but very loyal to his friends, even if his friends were few'. Both of the Wright brothers had been educated at what is now St Peter's School in York, where they would have met a local lad of their own age, Guy Fawkes.

Their sister Martha had married Thomas Percy, a young gentleman who was doing very well for himself. Percy, born in 1560, was second cousin to Henry Percy, ninth Earl of Northumberland (stories that he was the Earl's illegitimate half-brother have been discounted). Turning to

Tesimond again, we find that Percy was rather wild in his youth, 'a man who relied much on his sword and personal courage'. But he had quietened down as he matured, and had embraced Catholicism sincerely, and 'then changed his ways in remarkable fashion, giving much satisfaction to the Catholics and considerable cause for wonder to those who had known him previously'. Percy was tall and well-built, 'serious in countenance but with a pleasant manner', according to the proclamation which was to be issued for his arrest on 5 November 1605 a dark-haired and bearded man who was already greying. One sign of his growing maturity was that he was placed in a position of trust by his kinsman Northumberland in 1595, when he was made responsible for collecting the Earl's rents on his northern estates, and further acknowledgement of his capabilities came in the following year, when the Earl made him Constable of Alnwick Castle, a stronghold on the Scottish border. But there is also evidence that his youthful wildness persisted. Percy got into a number of scrapes (he was briefly imprisoned for killing a Scot in some border fracas) and was also sued for dishonesty by Northumberland's tenants; his personal life was also questionable, as there were strong suggestions that he was a bigamist. He was certainly estranged from Martha Wright, sister of John and Christopher Wright, whom he had married in 1591. By 1605 she, together with their daughter, was living on an annuity provided by the Catholic nobleman Lord Mounteagle (divorce in its modern sense did not exist in this period). The identity of his second 'spouse' remains uncertain, as does the status of their liaison.

Yet it remains clear that he retained the trust of the Earl of Northumberland. This nobleman enjoyed an ambivalent reputation in matters of religion. He was the nephew of the

Earl of Northumberland who had been executed after the 1569 Northern Rising, and one of his main objectives was to restore the Percy family's fortunes, both politically and financially (which might, perhaps, explain his apparent countenancing of Thomas Percy's rough way with his tenants). But he was also widely regarded, by both Catholics and their Protestant enemies, as a supporter of the Catholic cause, and himself described by a French ambassador as 'Catholic in his soul'. At the very least, Northumberland regarded himself as a natural protector of England's Catholics (his father, as well as his executed uncle, had been a staunch Catholic). Like all political players around 1600, Northumberland was aware that the aged Elizabeth did not have long to live, and decided to enter negotiations with her most obvious successor, James VI, King of Scotland, a known Protestant, on behalf of the Catholic interest. The man he sent to open these delicate negotiations was his kinsman Thomas Percy. Percy's efforts, ultimately, were fruitless: James, cautiously testing the political climate in the kingdom he was about to enter, was happy to discuss the problems of English Catholics, but was unwilling to make them any firm promises. But being sent on this mission, apparently, did nothing to lower Thomas Percy's self-esteem.

Another important personality in the English Catholic world of the late sixteenth century who was to become enmeshed in the Gunpowder Plot was Henry Garnett (or Garnet). Garnet was born in 1555 in Heanor in Derbyshire, and his family background was a solid one, his father being a man of some wealth and much learning who had taught at Nottingham Free School. Raised a Protestant, Garnett converted to Catholicism and, after working for a while in the workshop of a printer of law books, he went to Rome and eventually became a Jesuit. He was a man of considerable academic abilities, but despite feelings in the Society of Jesus that his talents would be better deployed in education and theology, he was sent to England as a missionary, landing there with another Jesuit, Robert Southwell, in July 1586. Shortly afterwards, on the imprisonment of the former holder of the position, William Weston, Garnett was made Superior of the Jesuits' English Province, a role he was to fulfil effectively for the next sixteen years. The description of him given in the proclamation of January 1606 ordering his arrest depicts him as 'of a middling stature, full faced, fat of body, of complexion fair', his hair thin on his head, and both his head hair and his beard grizzled, 'his gait upright, and comely for a fat man'. But the personality and intellectual ability of this overweight, balding sixty-year-old were respected even by his enemies. Presiding over his trial for treason in 1606 Attorney-General Sir Edward Coke (admittedly constructing a rhetoric of a talented man gone wrong) described him as 'by birth a gentleman, by education a scholar ... he hath many gifts and endowments of nature, by art learned, a good linguist'.

By the time Garnett became Superior, various political factions were jockeying to put themselves in a favourable position in anticipation of the change of monarch. In particular, the existing rivalry between Robert Devereux, Earl of Essex, and William Cecil, Lord Burghley, was exacerbated. Burghley was Elizabeth's chief minister, and had built up a formidable political machine which, after his death in 1598, was taken over by his son, Robert Cecil. Essex, born in 1567, was a favourite of the old school, a nobleman of dash and valour who had come to prominence late in Elizabeth's reign, winning fame and glory after leading a successful expedition against Cadiz in 1596. But his star was waning by the late 1590s: a second expedition against Spain was unsuccessful, and in 1599 Essex was appointed Lord Lieutenant of Ireland, where his performance was disastrous in both political and military terms. Sensing that the tide was running against him, he rallied together other young men who felt themselves marginalised by the political influence of Cecil. Among these were a number of Catholic gentlemen who hoped that their support would encourage the Earl, should he prove successful, to grant their co-religionists better conditions. On 8 February 1601 Essex and 200 men tried to mount a *coup d'état* in London, but attracted scant support. Essex was captured, tried for treason, and subsequently executed on 25 February. Many of those who supported him were also taken, a few executed, and several subjected to imprisonment and fines. Among these latter were Robert Catesby, John Wright and Francis Tresham. The fine laid upon Tresham was paid by his father, but Catesby (despite some assistance from the elder Tresham) had himself to pay most of the 5,000 marks fine levied upon him, and was forced to sell some of his property to do so. The young Catholic malcontent became even more embittered.

After the Essex Rebellion it became increasingly clear that the next ruler of England would be the Protestant James VI, King of Scotland. The English Catholic community awaited his accession with tempered optimism. The last years of Elizabeth's reign had been a relatively easy period for them, but England's Catholics had every reason to remember the fines, the hunts for seminary priests, the executions, the loss of civil liberties. They hoped for something better in the new reign. They were aware that in France the religious wars were over, and that the new French King, Henri IV, a Protestant turned Catholic, had, by the Edict of Nantes, guaranteed the right to worship and civil liberties of the Huguenots. It seemed feasible that this model could also apply to England's Catholics, while those with a broader knowledge of contemporary European affairs could point to Poland and Hungary, both of which were enjoying de facto religious toleration at the end of the sixteenth century. In the early hours of Thursday 24 March 1603 Elizabeth I died. For England's Catholics, so much depended on the new monarch.

2

THE PLOT

The accession of James VI of Scotland to the English throne was a remarkably smooth process. Many at the time had feared that it would not be. Sir Francis Bacon, Lord Chancellor of England and a well-informed observer of contemporary events, remembered how it had generally been anticipated that

> there must follow in England nothing but confusions, interreigns, and perturbations of estate; likely far to exceed the ancient calamities of the civil wars between the Houses of Lancaster and York, by how much more the dissensions were like to be more mortal and bloody when foreign competition should be added to domestical, and matter of religion to matter of title to the crown.

Had he known of it, Bacon's concerns would have been heightened by evidence that some of those outside the political elite had their own views on the change of monarch, sometimes expressing discontents which might be turned by factious great men to their own use. In September 1603, a few months after Elizabeth's death, a number of men were tried for seditious words at the Essex Summer Assizes at

Brentwood. One had voiced an extreme Protestant critique of the new monarch, another a Catholic one, a third was indicted for wishing that the Scots and the English 'had all of them gone together by the ears', adding that 'it was pity the king came so peaceably to this place', a fourth had allegedly declared that James, although proclaimed King of England, was not really such until he had been crowned, that there was no law until the King had enacted laws through Parliament, and 'that there were as wise men in England as to have been king as the king of Scots'. This suggests a wider discontent in local society which could so easily have fuelled a broader and deeper political instability. But in the event all went well. As Francis Bacon put it, 'it rejoices all men to see so fair a morning of a kingdom, and to be thoroughly secured of former apprehensions; as a man that awaketh out of a fearful dream'. But this rejoicing did not dispel the sense that James shared with his advisers that there was little room to be complacent about the viability of the new regime.

As James and these advisers were all too aware, there were a number of other people in March 1603 who might have felt they had as good a claim to the English crown as the King of Scots. James, as Elizabeth's cousin, had a strong claim in blood, just as his mother Mary Queen of Scots had had before him. But he was descended from the Scottish Tudor line which had not been mentioned in Henry VIII's will, which had governed the succession on three previous occasions, and so, it could be argued, was effectively excluded from it. By Henry's will the crown should have gone to Edward Seymour, Viscount Beauchamp, the son of Katherine Grey, who had inherited the rights of Henry's younger sister Mary. Arabella Stuart, whose father's grandmother had been the eldest Tudor princess, Margaret, Queen of Scotland after her

4. *Divine-right monarchy personified. James VI and I, King of Great Britain, as depicted in the frontispiece to his collected political works published in 1616. The ideological power mobilised by such imagery helps explain why contemplating tyrannicide was such a big step for the early modern mind.*

marriage to James IV in 1503, was another possible claimant. A rather more attenuated claim, but one which was of great interest to some of England's Catholics, was that of the Infanta Isabella of Spain, daughter of Philip II (who had died a few years previously) and sister of the reigning Spanish monarch, Philip III. She claimed to be a Plantagenet descended from John of Gaunt, although by 1603 a claim to the English throne on these grounds would not attract widespread support. As it was, James VI of Scotland emerged as the only viable candidate: quite apart from his strong claim in blood, he had the prerequisites necessary for success: he was male, adult, sane, had two sons and thus could guarantee the succession, and was also a Protestant.

The problem, both for England's Catholics and for her more extreme proponents of reformed religion, was exactly just what kind of Protestant he was. James's own religious beliefs were occasionally obscured by his tendency to adopt debating positions during theological discussions, while his views may have shifted in the last years of his life. In 1603, however, his position was fairly straightforward: he was a convinced Protestant of a more or less Calvinist cast of mind, intellectually hostile to Roman Catholicism, which he regarded as containing too many corruptions of true Christianity. Yet his pretensions to divine right monarchy had rendered the extreme Presbyterianism of the Scottish Kirk distasteful to him, and it was the knowledge of this, together with false hopes in James's leniency as the son of the 'martyred' Mary Queen of Scots, which encouraged English Catholics to expect better treatment under him (there were also rumours that his wife, Anne of Denmark, had adopted Catholicism). Moreover, James also fancied himself as a reconciler of disputes among Christians, and hoped for an eventual Protestant Christian unity which would be achieved by argument rather than force. Initially, therefore, he seems to have been disposed to ease the burdens on his new Catholic subjects. In his first speech to Parliament, on 19 March 1604, he told the assembled Lords and Commons that 'my mind was ever so free from persecution, or thralling of my subjects in matters of conscience, as I hope that those of that profession within this kingdom [i.e. Roman Catholicism] have a proof since my coming'. James had relaxed the laws against recusants, and fines coming into the Exchequer dropped markedly.

James is a monarch who has enjoyed an overwhelmingly bad press in traditional historiography, neatly lampooned in Sellars and Yeatman's pithy epigram, that 'James I slobbered at the mouth and had favourites: he was thus a bad king.' His reign is contrasted with the over-emphasised glories of the reign of Elizabeth, a monarch who, conversely, has enjoyed a very good press. James's reign has also frequently been portrayed as the stage at which Crown and Parliament took the first steps on the highroad to the civil wars which were to break out in 1642. And, of course, King Henri IV of France's comment, that James was the wisest fool in Christendom, is also usually thrown in. Modern re-assessments have created a more nuanced and more favourable impression. James's alleged mis-rule in England is contrasted with the fairly effective job he did on the rather more robust task of ruling Scotland, which suggests that those analysing his reign in England may have been asking the wrong questions. He did depend on favourites and faction, but until the rise of the Duke of Buckingham late in the reign, this dependency was normally kept under control. Perhaps his greatest, if understandable failing, noted from the very beginning of his reign, was to favour his Scottish courtiers: indeed, the reign of James I was to witness numerous early examples of that recurring figure in English history, the Scotsman on the make. The King's intellectual style, which has so often led to charges of pedantry against him, was typical of the period, and James emerges as that rarest of entities, a British monarch with serious pretensions to intellectual ability. And some indication of his political acumen can be gauged from the fact that, unlike his father, grandfather or mother, this 'wisest fool in Christendom' was to end his life by dying in bed at a decent age of natural causes. In this he was more fortunate than the author of that 'wisest fool in Christendom' jibe: in 1610, fifteen years before James's death, Henri IV joined the list of rulers assassinated by fanatical Catholics, in his case a young man named François Ravaillac.

Whatever James's personality, there can be little doubt that the smoothness of his succession owed much to somebody who is a pivotal character in the history of the Gunpowder Plot, Robert Cecil, from May 1605 Earl of Salisbury. Cecil, born about 1563, benefited immensely from being the son of Lord Burghley, Queen Elizabeth's first minister, the man who was, essentially, the architect of her greatness. Young Robert went through the usual types of service appropriate to an Elizabethan politician on an upward career track, but his father's death in 1598 left him isolated and in a parlous position in relation to the glamorous and seemingly unstoppable Earl of Essex, his late father's great adversary. Cecil is an enigmatic figure. He was, from birth, of a delicate constitution. As an adult, he was short (about five feet two), which prompted Elizabeth I to refer to him as her 'little elf', and James I to call him his 'pigmy' or his 'little beagle'. He also had a slight curvature of the spine, which encouraged the political lampoons of the time to describe him as a hunchback. One suspects that coping with all this caused Cecil much pain, and certainly a psycho-historian would find much of interest in his character. What we do know is that after his father's death he became dedicated to playing power politics, and did it rather well. Cecil, hard-headed and inscrutable, gradually built up his political networks as Essex committed the series of political miscalculations which were to end in his rising of February 1601 and his subsequent execution. After Essex's demise, Cecil made contact with James and gradually rendered himself indispensable to the realisation of James's objective of becoming King of England. After March 1603, Cecil's survival and that of James I were, for the politician at least, inseparable, and the future Earl very much followed his father's line on seeing Catholics as a major threat to the English state. He also inherited his father's awareness of the importance of building up good intelligence networks.

One of the major reasons for having these networks was the detection of plots against the regime, plots of the type which Burghley had been so successful in overturning. In the early months of his reign James and his advisers were especially watchful for any threat. One came almost immediately, in the summer of 1603, with a Catholic priest, William Watson, at its centre. Watson, a member of the regular clergy, had been heavily involved in the anti-Jesuit faction fighting of the last few years. He was incensed when he discovered that the new King was proposing no alleviation of the recusancy laws, and drew a number of malcontents, Catholic and Protestant alike, into his plot. This, in essence, was to gather as many Catholics as possible together in Greenwich on 24 June 1603 under the pretence of offering the King a petition for the better treatment of his Catholic subjects. The plan was to seize James and extort his consent to whatever was demanded. But information about the plot was disclosed to the Jesuit John Gerard, who relayed it to his provincial, Henry Garnett, who in turn informed the Privy Council, thus wrecking the conspiracy and ensuring the arrest of the ringleaders. In gratitude, James promised a Catholic deputation headed by the indefatigable Thomas Tresham that recusancy fines would not be collected, while in any case the importance of this, the so-called 'Bye Plot', was eclipsed by the 'Main Plot', a conspiracy by Protestant malcontents to supplant James with Arabella Stuart. But it was never quite forgotten that Catholics had been involved in the first serious conspiracy against James.

The aftermath of the Bye Plot brought temporary relief for English recusants, and a political victory for the Jesuits in England. The following summer, however, was to witness a major blow against the more militant English Catholics. One of the roles in which James I cast himself was that of peacemaker, and among the things he inherited from Elizabeth was a war against Spain. This war was popular with James's subjects, but the new King was opposed to it. He was aware that the conflict was not going well for England, and uncertain that any English interests would be served by its continuation. He may, as a proponent of divine right monarchy, have felt hostile to the notion of supporting Dutch rebels fighting against what he would have perceived as their lawful monarch. Above all, he was convinced that England could not afford to keep the war going financially. Spain, too, was financially exhausted, as her chief minister, the Duke of Lerma, was all too aware, while Philip II had died in 1598, to be followed by Philip III, a monarch much less imbued with crusading zeal against Protestantism. Accordingly, the

Treaty of London, signed in August 1604, brought an end to a generation of Anglo-Spanish conflict. It also ended any realistic hopes that English Catholic extremists may have had of their religion being forcibly reimposed in England with Spanish military assistance.

THE PLOT IS LAID

Writing the history of the Gunpowder Plot is a difficult undertaking. The main sources are all – inevitably perhaps – biased: there was the government version promulgated immediately after the Plot's discovery; two lengthy contemporary Catholic accounts, both of them written by priests, which are well informed but obviously slanted in a particular direction; and the confessions of the plotters themselves, some of them extracted after torture or at least acute psychological pressure, some of them skewed in hopes of protecting friends or family members. There is also a recurrent counter-history of the Plot, harking back to ideas which were being mooted in its immediate aftermath that the whole affair was concocted by the Earl of Salisbury to rally support for James I's new and uncertain regime. This interpretation has never quite gone away, although it has received scant support from most of the Plot's historians. Yet if this counter-history is discounted, and if room is left for argument on points of detail, and if adjustment is made for the spin in the various seventeenth-century accounts, the main lines of the history of the Gunpowder Plot are clear enough.

It is generally accepted that the Plot's inception can be traced to a meeting on Sunday 20 May 1604 at an inn called the Duck and Drake near the Strand in London. Those present were Robert Catesby, Thomas Winter, John Wright, Thomas

5. Guy Fawkes enters the historical record: a section from the parish register of St Michael-le-Belfrey, York, showing (third entry from the top) the record of the baptism of 'Guye Fawkes sone to Edward Fawkes' on 16 April 1570.

Percy, and somebody new to most of the conspirators, a tall, powerfully built, reddish-brown-haired Yorkshireman named Guy, or as he usually styled himself by this point, Guido Fawkes.

There were, apparently, two branches of the Fawkes family in sixteenth-century York, one definitely and the other probably associated with the Yorkshire village of Farnley. The branch from which Guy Fawkes was descended was less well documented, and our knowledge of it begins in the 1530s with William Fawkes, Guy's paternal grandfather. He had settled in the parish of St Michael-le-Belfrey, adjacent to York Minster, and made his living as a notary or proctor in the ecclesiastic courts: then, as now, York, with its Archbishop, was the administrative centre of the Church in the north of England. William married Ellen Haryngton, daughter of a substantial York merchant, and evidently lived a life of solid prosperity in the upper reaches of the city's society. He was Sheriff of York in 1531, Lord Mayor in 1536, and received further promotions in the ecclesiastical courts before his death, which occurred between 1558 and 1565. His elder son, Thomas, died around 1581, apparently unmarried and without issue. His younger son, Edward, married and settled in a house in Stonegate. His wife, Edith, was to bear four children. The first, Anne, died in November 1568, less than six weeks after she was baptised, and was followed by Guy, baptised in St Michael-le-Belfrey on 16 April 1570, another Anne, baptised in October 1572, and Elizabeth, baptised in May 1575. The name Guy was an uncommon one in the England of the time, but it seems to have enjoyed popularity in sixteenth-century York on account of the lasting fame of a late fifteenth-century local notable, Sir Guy Fairfax of Steeton.

Edward Fawkes followed his father as an ecclesiastical lawyer, and it seems incontrovertible that the young Guy was raised as a Protestant; he was certainly educated in York at what is now St Peter's School. But his father died in 1579, aged about forty-six, and Guy's mother subsequently remarried, to a gentleman named Dionis Baynbrigge (he sometimes appears in modern accounts as Denis Bainbridge) who lived in Scotton, a township in the Yorkshire parish of Farnham. Baynbrigge was a Catholic, and Scotton also contained Catholic branches of the Pulleyn and Percy families. This meant that Guy was soon moving in Catholic circles, and the interlocking kinship and friendship networks of the Baynbrigges, Percys and Pulleyns meant that he came to know the Wrights, Winters and Thomas Percy. Certainly by the time Guy came of age in 1591 he had converted to Catholicism. In that year he disposed of his property, and within a year or two left England to serve against the Protestant Dutch rebels with Spain's Army of Flanders in the Netherlands. The Netherlands were the period's great school for soldiering, and the Army of Flanders was, as we have already noted, an extremely effective military organisation. It was essentially an international force. In November 1591, shortly before Guy Fawkes joined it, its total strength of just over 62,000 men included among its infantry units nearly 22,000 Germans, some 18,871 Netherlanders, 2,421 Italians, 2,119 Burgundians, and 9,579 Spaniards. There were also 463 Britons.

Serving in the infantry of the Army of Flanders as a gentleman-ranker, as Guy Fawkes did, was popular and regarded as eminently honourable among the Spanish gentry, and was fairly common among the other 'nations'. The army's British troops included men with the now familiar surnames

of Catesby and Tresham. One Netherlandish civilian commented that gentlemen-rankers were 'the people who bear
the brunt of the battles and sieges, as we have seen on many
occasions, and who by their example oblige and enliven the
rest of the soldiers (who have less sense of duty) to stand
fast and fight with courage'. There is every indication that
Fawkes fitted this model. He was present at the taking of
Calais by the Archduke Albert in 1596, was promoted to
ensign (roughly equivalent to a second lieutenant in the
modern British army), was clearly well thought of by the
veteran English Catholic soldier Sir Thomas Stanley, and
by 1603 was being put forward for a captaincy. The English
Jesuit Oswald Tesimond (incidentally another former pupil
of St Peter's School in York) described the Fawkes of this
period in the following terms:

> He was a man of considerable experience as well as
> knowledge. Thanks to his prowess he had acquired con-
> siderable fame and name among the soldiers. He was also
> – something decidedly rare among soldiery, although
> it was immediately evident to all – a very devout man,
> of exemplary life and commendable reticence. He went
> often to the sacraments. He was pleasant of approach
> and cheerful of manner, opposed to quarrels [i.e. duel-
> ling] and strife: a friend, at the same time, of all in the
> service with him who were men of honour and good life.
> In a word, he was a man liked by everyone and loyal to
> his friends.

One finds oneself instinctively in sympathy with the comment
of Francis Edwards, the translator of Tesimond's account of
the Gunpowder Plot, and himself a Jesuit, that 'one could

CONCILIVM SEPTEM NOBILIVM ANGLORVM CONIVRANTIVM IN NECEM IACOBI ·I· MAGNÆ BRITANNIÆ REGIS TOTIVSQ ANGLICI CONVOCATI PARLEMENTI

Christopher Wright
Iohn Wright
Robert Winter
Thomas Percy
Guido Fawkes
Robert Catesby
Thomas Winter
Bates

6. The central group of the conspirators, from a print of 1606. We have no way of telling how accurate a portrayal of the Gunpowder Plotters it is, but it does leave us with a lasting impression of the plot's key members.

wish for more confirmation of ... [this] glowing account': even so, this view of Guy Fawkes as the ardent Christian soldier is a currently widely accepted one. At the very least, the fact that he was entrusted by Sir William Stanley and the Welsh recusant émigré Hugh Owen to go on an unofficial mission to Spain on behalf of England's Catholics suggests that Fawkes was a man of unusual abilities. Tradition has it that among these abilities was expertise with gunpowder and explosives, expertise which one might plausibly have expected Fawkes to have acquired in the Netherlands.

Such expertise was clearly seen as desirable by Catesby as he revealed his plans to the other conspirators in the Duck and Drake that Sunday in 1604. He had decided, he told them, to blow up King and Parliament with gunpowder. Parliament, remarked Catesby, referring to the recusancy laws, was the place from whence all the mischief against England's Catholics had originated, and hence it was a logical and legitimate target for Catholics wanting to take direct action against their oppressors. Thomas Winter expressed his opposition to this scheme, pointing out, with considerable common sense, that if it failed the probable consequence would be a terrible worsening of the Catholics' position. Apparently the charismatic Catesby talked him round. Wright and Percy, more impulsive and fancying themselves as men of action, needed little persuading: Percy's opening words, we are told, were, 'Shall we always, gentlemen, talk and never do anything?' After more discussion, all five men swore an oath of secrecy on a prayerbook. The inn was apparently a Catholic safe house, for, it being a Sunday, Father John Gerard was celebrating Mass in another room there, and the five men took communion. The government was later to make much of this, claiming that this demonstrated a priestly blessing and endorsement of the Plot. There is, however, no reason to believe that Gerard had any idea of what the five gentlemen had been up to, and those of them who survived to be interrogated and executed were insistent on this point.

Once the plan put forward by Catesby had been accepted by his four confederates, the problem was now how to put it into operation. The plotters had an unexpected stroke of good fortune a few weeks later, on 9 June, when the Earl of Northumberland, Thomas Percy's patron and kinsman, used his influence to have him appointed a Gentleman Pensioner. The Gentlemen Pensioners were a body of fifty men founded under Henry VIII in 1539 as a life-guard for the monarch. From the start their function was mainly decorative. They provided a showy escort for the monarch (for example, they flanked James I in March 1604 when the retreat of the plague in London finally allowed the new monarch to process through his capital), and being a Gentleman Pensioner was a splendid opportunity for social advancement for young men of good family. After the Plot's discovery, Thomas Percy's social advancement was to have severe implications for Northumberland. Gentlemen Pensioners should on appointment have sworn the Oath of Allegiance, which among other things recognised the monarch as the supreme governor of the Church in England. Northumberland waived this requirement for Percy, probably because he knew the younger man to be a Catholic. This omission was to lead to the Earl being heavily fined and imprisoned for fifteen years for complicity in the Plot. But more immediately, the new appointment gave Percy a good reason to establish a base in London, and he selected a small dwelling in the precincts of Westminster, adjacent to the House of Lords and with easy access to the Thames. This belonged to John Whynniard, Keeper of the King's Wardrobe, but it was leased to a recusant, the antiquarian Henry Ferrers, who was happy to sublet it to Percy. Guy Fawkes was placed there in the guise of a servant of Percy's acting as a caretaker, and adopted the alias of John Johnson. Catesby had a house at Lambeth, on the south bank of the Thames, and it was intended that gunpowder and other necessaries should be kept there and ferried across the river to Westminster. Probably early in October a recusant named Robert Keyes was installed in the house and put in charge of this part of the operation. Keyes, who had inherited his Catholicism from his mother, a member of the Tyrrwhitts, a well-known recusant family in Lincolnshire, was aged about forty, and regarded as a trustworthy man who was likely to show courage in a crisis. A little later, probably in early December 1604, Thomas Bates was brought into the

Plot. Bates was Catesby's trusted servant, although the fact that he was allowed his own armour and permitted to have a servant of his own suggests that he was no mere menial.

The plotters considered how to secure a Catholic England in the wake of the destruction of King, Lords and Commons. They calculated that total confusion would follow such a blow, and envisaged a general recusant rising. They planned to use as a figurehead for the rising Princess Elizabeth, James I's third child, who was to attain her eighth birthday in August 1604. This, they felt, would add legitimacy to their cause, and in any case, effective control would pass to a Protector, whose exact identity was undecided but who would be selected or would emerge from among England's Catholic peers. The young princess lived at Combe Abbey, near Coventry. Hence involvement of nearby Catholic gentry, well positioned to secure the young princess, in the Plot became a necessary component of the next stage in its planning. This in turn necessitated a broadening of the number of plotters. In March 1605 Thomas Winter's brother Robert, John Wright's brother Christopher, and another Warwickshire gentleman, John Grant, were brought into the conspiracy. Grant's home at Norbrook was a well-established hiding-place for Catholic priests, and was strategically positioned to act as a centre for the projected rising. Later in the year, new confederates were recruited. At the end of September 1605 the young and wealthy recusant gentleman Ambrose Rookwood, who had already been involved in supplying gunpowder to the plotters under the pretence that it was destined for pro-Habsburg troops in Flanders, was recruited as a conspirator. He was famous for his stable of fine horses, potential cavalry mounts for the Catholic insurgents. Francis Tresham, son of the noted Sir

Thomas, was recruited a little later, probably on the basis of his family's reputation in Catholic circles and its (admittedly now rather diminished) wealth. Tresham, however, was a reluctant plotter, and there have been strong suspicions that he betrayed the conspiracy to Salisbury. And lastly, and not very long before the projected coup, the young and gallant Sir Everard Digby was brought in to be coordinator of the Midlands rising, although he was not, at this stage, given full details of what the Plot involved. With Digby's recruitment, the conspirators reached their final total, an unpropitious thirteen.

While the network of Midland gentry supporters was being built up, operations in London continued, despite the frustrations attendant upon constant prorogations of Parliament. The plotters apparently planned to dig a tunnel and plant explosives under the Houses of Parliament, an inherently unlikely strategy and one which was in any case rendered unnecessary when, in March 1605, they obtained the lease to a storeroom belonging to Whynniard's dwelling which was located on the ground floor under the House of Lords. Dirty and unkempt, essentially a place where coal and firewood was stored, it was ideal for the conspirators' purposes. Percy bargained with Whynniard (or, to be more accurate, Whynniard's wife) under the pretext that he needed it because his own wife was planning to join him in London. Over the next few months, thirty-six barrels of powder were assembled in this storeroom, which has passed into history as 'Guy Fawkes's cellar'. It is surprising that private individuals were able to assemble so much explosive without attracting official attention, but the conspirators had the necessary connections and, in any case, the end of the war against Spain had created something of a buyer's market for gunpowder. Rather more serious, from the plotters' point of view, was the tendency for the component elements in gun-powder to separate, necessitating its remixtuure. Here Guy Fawkes's knowledge of powder and its employment was vital.

The nature of the Palace of Westminster also helped the conspirators to assemble so much powder under the House of Lords without being detected. The Palace, as recent his-torian of the Plot, Antonia Fraser, has put it, 'was a warren of meeting-rooms, semi-private chambers, apartments – and commercial enterprises of all sorts ... there were taverns, wine-merchants, a baker's shop in the same block as the Whynniard lodging, booths and shops everywhere'. There was nothing like a modern security system around Westminster, and, indeed, little by way of policing of any sort. It seems that Salisbury's informants sensed something was afoot, and certainly after the Plot had been discovered Salisbury was to claim that intelligence which reached him had led him to suspect a Catholic 'stir' of some sort. But there had been false rumours of Catholic Plots before, while the plotters themselves maintained a high level of security. Guy Fawkes went over to Flanders in the spring of 1605 in a final effort to raise Habsburg support, and one of Salisbury's agents noted his presence there, Fawkes's name thus appear-ing in the Earl's intelligence system for the first time. But there was, of course, nothing to associate Guy Fawkes with Thomas Percy's servant John Johnson. So when Fawkes, now returned to England, went to carry out what was meant to be a penultimate check in Whynniard's storeroom on 30 October 1605, he had every reason to believe that the Plot was undetected and stood a good chance of success. By that date, however, a train of events had been set in motion which ensured that the Plot would fail, and that all thirteen conspirators would die for their involvement.

THE PLOT UNRAVELS

William Parker, Lord Mounteagle, was a young nobleman who, like other peers, was intending to attend Parliament when it sat on 5 November. He had been a Catholic in the previous reign, and, like so many other young malcontents, had been involved in the Essex rebellion. But on the accession of James to the English throne he promised to conform to the Church of England. His wife, however, remained a recusant, while Mounteagle had a broader circle of kinsfolk, friends and contacts in the Catholic community. According to the government's version of the Gunpowder Plot story, on the evening of 26 October a servant of Mounteagle's, Thomas Ward, a Yorkshire recusant related to John and Christopher Wright, was stopped by 'an unknown man of reasonable tall personage'. This 'unknown man' gave Ward a letter to deliver to his master, who was at dinner in his house at Hoxton, then on the fringes of London. Mounteagle had difficulty in deciphering the letter, and called Ward to help him read it by candlelight. The two men rapidly realised that they had before them a disturbing if puzzling piece of documentation. The letter, its English modernised, ran as follows:

My Lord out of the love I bear to some of your friends I have a care of your preservation. Therefore I would advise you as you tender your life to devise some excuse to shift off your attendance at this Parliament, for God and man hath concurred to punish the wickedness of this time. And think not slightly of this advertisement but retire yourself into your country [i.e. county, home area] where you may expect the event in safety, for though there be no appearance of any stir yet I say they shall receive a terrible blow this parliament and yet they shall not see who hurts them. This counsel is not to be contemned because it may do you good and can do you no harm for the danger is passed as soon as you have burnt the letter and I hope God will give you the grace to make good use of it to whose holy protection I commend you.

Mounteagle did not burn the letter. Instead, either out of loyalty to James's regime or out of fear that he might be implicated in any 'stir' which did occur (and Mounteagle, through his contacts with the recusant community, was better placed than most to hear such rumours of Catholic plots as were circulating), he took it straight to Whitehall, where he found the Earls of Salisbury, Suffolk, Worcester, Nottingham and Northampton on the point of sitting down to dine. Mounteagle requested a few words in private with Salisbury and, this being granted, told him what had happened. Salisbury appears initially to have been sceptical about the reality of any threat hinted at in the letter, and he certainly waited until 1 November, the day after James had returned from a hunting expedition, to tell the King about it.

It was the Mounteagle letter that scuppered the Gunpowder Plot, and much ink has been spilt over its authorship. At the time there were strong suppositions, on what basis it is now unclear, that the author was Thomas Percy, but the most likely candidate was Francis Tresham, who, as we have seen, had reservations about the Plot and

7. The discovery of the Mounteagle letter, from Francis Herring's
Mischeefes Mysterie *of 1617, an English translation of a verse history of
the plot first published in its immediate aftermath. In a heavy allegory, an
eagle gives a sealed copy of the letter to the Earl of Salisbury, while James
stretches his hand out to receive it.*

who was also, through the nobleman's marriage to his
sister Elizabeth, Mounteagle's brother-in-law. In fact, the
author of the letter has never been definitively identified,
and as one recent writer on the Plot has commented, 'many
names both probable and improbable have been suggested',
among them Salisbury himself, the Jesuit Edward Oldcorne,
Thomas Phelippes (a cryptographer and intelligence agent),
Mounteagle's sister Mary Habington of Hindlip, Thomas
Winter, the recusant gentlewoman Anne Vaux, and Francis
Tresham's servant William Vavasour. A book wholly devoted
to the subject, published in 1901, arguing that the letter was

written by the Jesuit Edward Oldcorne at Thomas Winter's instigation with heavy involvement from Mounteagle's servant Thomas Ward, gives the impression that the author was trying to get an obsession out of his system. More recently, and more plausibly, Antonia Fraser has argued that the letter was actually written at Mounteagle's command, immediately after he had been warned verbally, probably by Tresham, about the Plot. Certainly, Mounteagle did very well as a result of his revelations: he received lands worth £200 a year and a pension of £500 for his services to the state, and he arose unsullied from the wreckage of a conspiracy in which a number of his friends, relatives and acquaintances had been involved.

Thomas Ward, Mounteagle's servant, contacted the plotter Thomas Winter and told him of the letter, and Winter did his best to persuade Catesby that the Plot should be discontinued. But Catesby decided that the letter was too unspecific to constitute a real threat, and in fact persuaded Winter and the others that they should continue as planned. One man who did take the letter seriously was James I. On 4 November, at the King's insistence, a party headed by the Earl of Suffolk and including Mounteagle searched the area around the Palace of Westminster. Suffolk, while not wishing to disquiet the 'very tall and desperate fellow' who appeared to be looking after it, was surprised by the amount of firewood in one of the storerooms under the Palace, and he and his associates were even more surprised to discover that the cellar's tenant was Thomas Percy. James, on being informed of this, ordered a second search, this time to be headed by the reliable Sir Thomas Knyvett, Keeper of Whitehall Palace, member of the King's Privy Chamber, and a justice of the peace for Westminster. Either shortly before midnight on 4 November or in the early hours of the following morning, Knyvett and his party returned to the storeroom rented by Percy and discovered its attendant wearing a cloak and booted and spurred as if anticipating imminent departure. Knyvett ordered him to be arrested, and, probing among the firewood, found numerous barrels of gunpowder. The attendant, who gave his name as John Johnson, was searched, and fuses, or 'matches' as the seventeenth century termed them, and tubes to pass them through, were found about his person. An extra guard was put in place, privy councillors were woken up, and within a few hours a royal proclamation had been issued which declared Thomas Percy a traitor and called for his arrest. The Gunpowder Plot had been discovered.

What all accounts agree on is the total courage with which Guy Fawkes faced his initial interrogation. A gentleman named Edward Hoby, writing on 19 November to Sir Thomas Edmondes, the English ambassador at Brussels, told how when Fawkes was brought into the King's presence James 'asked him how he could conspire so hideous a treason against his children and so many innocent souls which never offended him?' Fawkes replied that this was true, 'but a dangerous disease required a desperate remedy'. Moreover, touching on the Scotophobia which was prevalent among the English early in James's reign, Fawkes 'told some of the Scots that his intent was to have blown them back to Scotland'. Hoby added that at this stage 'yet was his countenance so far from being dejected, as he often smiled in scornful manner, not only avowing the fact, but repenting only his failing in the execution thereof, whereof, he said, the devil, not God, was the discoverer'. James, it seemed, was impressed by Fawkes's courage. This did not prevent the

King from authorising the use of torture in 'John Johnson's' interrogation.

Torture is something which can usually be depended upon to break courage. England at this time favoured two main forms of torture when interrogating supposed traitors. The first was the manacles. These were iron gloves into which the hands of the suspect were placed, and from which he was hung up against a wall. He would stand on a pile of wooden billets, which would gradually be kicked away from under him, to leave him dangling, sometimes for several hours. The gauntlets could also be tightened to heighten the agony. And then there was the rack, on which the body of the suspect would be stretched, a torture which resulted in dislocations of the arms and legs and usually caused permanent physical harm. Fawkes was definitely subjected to the manacles, and in all probability to the rack. He held out, as far as we can tell, until late on 7 November, and then began to talk, over the next two days gradually giving more evidence, and naming names, after each bout of torture. The signature on his final confession, compared to that on the first, tells the story of a man who had been physically and mentally broken.

Initially, the only suspect whom the authorities could name was the master of the supposed 'John Johnson', Thomas Percy. But even before Fawkes had cracked, government efforts, especially those of Sir John Popham, Lord Chief Justice and a man with contacts, and apparently informants, among London's recusant community, had identified a wider network of conspirators. Accordingly, by a Proclamation of 7 November Robert Catesby, Ambrose Rookwood, Thomas Winter, Edward Grant, John Wright, Christopher Wright and Robert Ashfield (an alias for Bates) were added to the list of traitors to be hunted down. Robert Winter, Francis Tresham,

Sir Everard Digby and Robert Keyes had yet to be identified as suspects.

Naturally enough most of the plotters who had been in London on 5 November – notably Christopher Wright, Thomas Winter and Thomas Percy – left the capital as soon as they knew that the Plot had been discovered (as might be imagined, the news caused considerable uproar) and headed for the Midlands. Leaving the country might have been thought more sensible, but Catesby, characteristically, decided to go down fighting, and, again characteristically, persuaded his co-conspirators to do the same. Unfortunately, the hoped-for groundswell of recusant support proved unforthcoming. Sir Everard Digby had arranged a meeting of a number of Midland recusant gentlemen, ostensibly for a hunting party at Dunchurch near Rugby, but most of them headed home when they learnt what the real purpose of their coming together was, and many of those who joined the rising initially defected within a few hours. Not only were the conspirators failing to rouse support among recusant laymen, their actions failed to attract any approval from Catholic priests. Catesby sent a letter to Henry Garnett asking him to help foment a rising among recusants in Wales, an idea which dismayed the Jesuit, while on 7 November the Archpriest Father Blackwell published a forceful condemnation of the Plot, trying as strongly as was possible to disassociate mainstream Catholics from so dreadful an enterprise. He described it as a 'detestable device', declared it unlawful for 'private subjects, by private authority, to take arms against their lawful king', and urged Catholic priests to instruct their flocks to this effect. On Blackwell's prompting, Pope Paul V was to issue a statement to the same effect on 28 November.

After trailing around various recusant gentry houses in the vain hope of raising support, at about ten in the evening of 7 November the small band of conspirators reached Holbeach House in Staffordshire, home of Stephen Littleton, one of the few members of Digby's hunting-party who was still with them. Again they failed to rouse any support from their local recusant contacts, and resolved to make what most of them knew would be a last stand there. But even before the arrival of government forces, another disaster befell them. They had taken a cartload of arms and gunpowder in their journeyings, and the gunpowder had been drenched by heavy rain. With massive foolhardiness, they had spread this out in front of an open fire to dry. The powder was ignited by a spark from the fire and exploded, blinding John Grant and injuring another member of the hunting-party, Henry Morgan. Everard Digby had already departed with the intention of giving himself up, Catesby's servant Thomas Bates had also gone, while Stephen Littleton, who had been away with Thomas Winter trying to drum up local support, decided to flee when he heard about the explosion at Holbeach House. The group remaining in the house thus consisted of Catesby, Thomas Percy, Thomas Winter, John and Christopher Wright, the injured Henry Morgan, the blinded John Grant and Ambrose Rookwood, who had also been scorched and shaken by the gunpowder explosion. Their chances were therefore negligible when the Sheriff of Worcestershire, Sir Richard Walsh, arrived with a force of some 200 men.

The Gunpowder Plot ended with a brief fight at Holbeach House on Friday 8 November. Many of Walsh's men were equipped with arquebuses, and they used them to good effect. Thomas Winter was shot in the shoulder, and deprived of the use of his right arm, at the very beginning of the engagement, and John and Christopher Wright were hit soon afterwards, as was Ambrose Rookwood. Catesby and the wounded Thomas Winter, those two old friends, made their last stand together, along with Thomas Percy, at the door of Holbeach House. Catesby and Percy were brought down together by the same bullet, fired by a Worcester man, John Streete: he was later to petition for £1,000 as a reward for this feat, which, given the accuracy of seventeenth-century firearms, surely owed more to luck than marksmanship. The sheriff's men, excited by the chase and their victory, then rushed the house and began to strip the bodies of the dead and wounded, this maltreatment ensuring the deaths of the badly wounded Wright brothers and Thomas Percy. Grant, Morgan and Rookwood were captured without too much trouble. Robert Catesby, mortally wounded, already wearing a gold crucifix, managed to crawl into the interior of the house, where he found a picture of the Virgin Mary which he was holding in his arms when he died. Sir Thomas Lawley, who was helping Walsh, had Catesby's crucifix and the picture sent to London as symbols of popish superstition.

Thomas Bates, a fugitive from Holbeach House, was apprehended in Staffordshire, while Robert Keyes was also picked up. The dashing young gentleman Everard Digby, on his way to give himself up to a friend in Warwickshire, was caught by a posse along with two of his servants. Francis Tresham was arrested in London on the basis of evidence supplied under torture by Guy Fawkes. Robert Winter, on the run with Stephen Littleton, was eventually captured in Worcestershire on 9 January 1606. The government had already begun to extend its investigations beyond the original plotters. In particular, a number of Catholic peers were

8. The death of Catesby at Holbeach House, as imagined by George Cruikshank. In this depiction, as in reality, Catesby died a good Catholic.

imprisoned, for the government was convinced that so serious a threat to the regime had to have a nobleman behind it. The Earl of Northumberland, the patron of Thomas Percy, in whose rented premises the gunpowder had been placed, and a known supporter of the Catholic interest, was an obvious suspect, and was imprisoned first at the Archbishop of Canterbury's palace at Lambeth and transferred to the Tower of London on 27 November. By that time three other Catholic peers with connections with the Plot, Lords Montague, Mourdant and Stourton, were already there: we must sympathise with Montague, who attracted suspicion largely because he had briefly employed Guy Fawkes to wait at his table. And the government wanted to spread the net yet further. It was impossible to imagine a Catholic plot in which no Catholic priests were involved. Gerard and Tesimond escaped from England, the latter as a stowaway on a boat carrying pig carcasses to Calais, and both were later to write accounts of the conspiracy. Garnett, to the delight of the government, was captured on 27 January 1606 after hiding for eight days in a priest's hole in the Catholic safehouse at Hindlip in Worcestershire. The authorities finally had a Jesuit to try and execute.

That, then, was the story of the Gunpowder Plot. It was essentially a failed act of terrorism in which thirteen men, most of them born into the gentry or a similar social level, all of them with a strong Catholic faith, were involved. We might well speculate on what would have happened if Guy Fawkes had ignited the thirty-six barrels of gunpowder, and if a serious recusant rising in the Midlands had led to the seizure of Princess Elizabeth and the setting up of a Catholic regime headed by the Earl of Northumberland or some other noble Catholic 'Protector'. But the Plot, despite the audacity

9. Guy Fawkes entering the Houses of Parliament, with the powder barrels just discernible: a detail from a print of 1621. As one of the captions reminds us, this was a deed of darkness.

of its conception, failed, and the nature of its failure, among other things, demonstrated just how illusory the Catholic threat as imagined by Protestant Englishmen really was. The authorities were now left with the task of trying the eight surviving plotters, the handful of provincial recusants who had rallied to their cause, and Garnett the Jesuit.

3

REMEMBERING THROUGH THE

SEVENTEENTH CENTURY

TRIAL, EXECUTION AND THE BEGINNING OF REMEMBERING

The trial of the eight surviving conspirators was held in Westminster Hall (which would have been destroyed had the Plot been successful) on Monday 27 January 1606. The Commissioners trying them consisted of the Earls of Nottingham, Suffolk, Worcester, Devonshire, Northampton and Salisbury, along with Lord Chief Justice Sir John Popham, Thomas Fleming, Lord Chief Baron of the Exchequer, and Sir Peter Warburton, one of the Justices of the Common Pleas. Of those on trial, Robert Winter, Thomas Winter, John Grant, Ambrose Rookwood, Robert Keyes, Thomas Bates and Guy Fawkes pleaded not guilty, while Sir Everard Digby decided to plead guilty, apparently on the assumption that this would allow him to make a speech before the court explaining his conduct.

Directing the prosecution was the Attorney General, Sir Edward Coke. Coke was one of the most eminent lawyers of his day, author of several books on the English Common Law and a man who enjoyed a dazzlingly successful career. He had presided over the trials of the Earl of Essex in 1601 and Sir Walter Raleigh two years later, and was an obvious choice to mastermind what was intended to be a show trial

10. Sir Edward Coke (1552–1634), who presided over the trials of the plotters and Henry Garnett. Coke is one of the heroes of the English Common Law tradition, and he was involved in a number of other political trials in this period, notably those of the Earl of Essex and Sir Walter Raleigh.

of massive significance. The Attorney General treated his listeners to a lengthy speech which both, via a plethora of classical, biblical and legal references, demonstrated his learning, and left those present, and those who were later to read the printed version of his oration, in no doubt about the enormity of the crime which the gunpowder conspirators had envisaged. Their offences constituted 'the greatest treasons that ever were plotted in England, and concern the greatest King that ever was of England', treasons intended not just to kill the King but also to destroy the whole English polity, a crime *'sine exemplo,* beyond all examples, whether in fact or fiction, even of the tragick poets, who did beat their wits to represent the most fearful and horrible murders'. Coke offered a short narrative of the Plot, and, as might be expected, reminded the court of previous Catholic conspiracies, arguing that the Gunpowder Plot arose 'out of the ashes of dead treasons', and also claimed that Catholic governments in Spain and the Hapsburg Low Countries were implicated. But perhaps the most powerful message that Coke tried to convey was the central and corrosive influence of the Jesuits. 'The principal offenders,' he declared, 'are the seducing Jesuits; men that use the reverence of religion, yea, even the most sacred and blessed name of Jesus, as a mantle to cover their impiety, blasphemy, treason and rebellion, all manner of wickedness', which included their commitment to 'deposing of kings, and disposing of kingdoms'.

Sir Everard Digby was allowed his speech. In it he pleaded that he acted not out of malice to King or Parliament, but rather out of friendship to Catesby. He also explained his conduct through his religious convictions in general, to which was added resentment that what he perceived as promises made to England's Catholics by James had been reneged on,

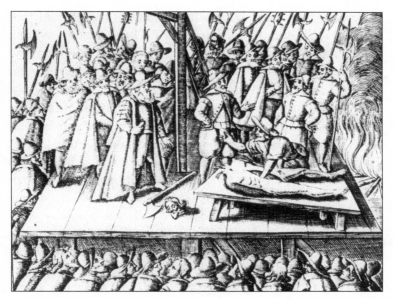

11. The execution of the plotters. This print of 1606 displays the final stages of hanging, drawing and quartering at their most gruesome. The executioner, having beheaded and cut the arms off one of those executed, is showing his heart to the presiding officer. The fire to the right was for burning the entrails and genitals of the dead: the process of hanging, drawing and quartering involved castration and disembowelment.

and that he feared harsher laws against recusants. He also pleaded that were he to be convicted of treason, his family should not, as the law dictated, also suffer, and that given his social status he should be executed by beheading, as befitted a gentleman. None of this cut any ice with the court. Coke and others rebutted his explanations of his conduct, and both his requests were denied. At the end of proceedings, all eight accused were found guilty of treason, and sentenced to death by hanging, drawing and quartering.

Executions for treason in this period, like most other

punishments, were carried out in public. The convicted conspirators were to die in two groups: Digby, Robert Winter, Grant and Bates in St Paul's churchyard on Thursday 30 January; Rookwood, Thomas Winter, Keyes and Fawkes in the Old Palace Yard at Westminster on the following day. The first stage of the theatre of punishment for traitors (other than noblemen) was that they should be dragged from prison to the place of execution on a hurdle, usually made of wickerwork, since, as Coke expressed it at their trial, a traitor was 'not worthy any more to tread upon the face of the earth whereof he was made'. The streets between the prisons where the plotters were held and the sites where they were to be executed were packed on those two cold January days, and as the condemned were dragged to their deaths there occurred a number of incidents which must have affected even the most hardened anti-Catholics. There is a tradition that one of Sir Everard Digby's sons, although many miles away, called out 'tata, tata' at the precise moment of his father's execution. Martha Bates, wife of Thomas Bates, managed to evade the soldiers who were lining the route, threw herself on the hurdle carrying her husband, and wept as she held him (Bates, a hardheaded man, apparently took the opportunity to tell her the location of some hidden money). Elizabeth Rookwood so positioned herself that she could watch her husband being dragged past from the window of their lodgings in the Strand. When he reached the spot, Rookwood cried to his wife, 'Pray for me, pray for me!' 'I will, and be of good courage,' she replied, recommending him to offer himself up to God.

'Good courage' was a commodity of which any male commoner undergoing death for treason in Stuart England was in dire need. Sir Edward Coke's speech again:

12. By way of a contrast to the last illustration, the execution of Guy Fawkes as depicted in 1841 by George Cruikshank. The execution of the plotters has been suitably sanitised by the early Victorian period.

... he shall be strangled, being hanged up by the neck between heaven and earth, as deemed unworthy of both or either: as likewise, that the eyes of men may behold, and their hearts condemn him. Then he is to be cut down alive, and to have his privy parts cut off and burnt before his face as being unworthily begotten, and unfit to leave any generation after him. His bowels and inlaid parts taken out and burnt, who inwardly had conceived and harboured in his heart such horrible treason. After, to have his head cut off, which had imagined the mischief. And lastly his body to be quartered, and the quarters set up in some high and eminent place, to the view and detestation of men, and to become a prey for the fowls of the air.

Such accounts as we have agree that traitors on the scaffold usually showed great bravery in the face of what was about to happen to them, and the Gunpowder conspirators were no exception. Digby, the first to be executed, made a courageous speech, declaring that his religion left him with a clear conscience, although he admitted that he had broken the laws of his country. He said goodbye to those of the great and the good who were present with whom he had been acquainted, and left the audience impressed by his fortitude. Thomas Bates, several rungs down the social scale, gave a more muted farewell speech, attributing his conduct to misplaced loyalty to his master Robert Catesby, and asking forgiveness of all those present. Guy Fawkes was the last to die. Probably broken by torture and sickness, he did not speak at length, but merely asked forgiveness from the King and his people. He then had to be helped up the ladder before being hanged. Fortunately, he mounted high enough to break his neck when he was turned off, and hence was spared the agony of the ritual mutilation of his body which followed. All eight of the conspirators died Catholic.

A few more executions followed in the provinces, notably those of men who had been involved in the abortive rising which had ended so tragically at Holbeach House. But the government was to be allowed one final show trial and public execution: Henry Garnett the Jesuit, who had been captured in Worcestershire on the day that the conspirators were tried, 27 January. As Coke's speech at the trial of the conspirators had made plain, the government was convinced of the involvement of the Jesuits in the Plot, and a warrant, complete with descriptions, had been issued for the arrest of Garnett, John Gerard and Oswald Tesimond. Garnett was, however, the most important catch. Ironically, he had been horrified by the Plot and had argued against it, realising that, leaving its morality aside, it would probably fail and bring a terrifying retribution down on England's Catholic minority. But few Protestant Englishmen were likely to believe that a Jesuit would adopt such a position, while Garnett was far from entirely free from guilt, under English law at least. In July 1605 Tesimond, under the seal of the confession, had told Garnett how Catesby had, in his turn, at an earlier point, confessed details of the Plot to him. Thus Garnett knew about the conspiracy, but his position as a Catholic priest meant that he was unable to pass on details of treason which had been relayed to him under confession. The logic was unbreakable given his status as a Catholic priest, but his status as a subject of King James meant that he was guilty of misprision of treason, that is, knowing that treason was about to be committed and being unwilling to relay the details to the authorities.

Coke, presiding over Garnett's trial on Friday 28 March 1606, made another setpiece speech. He began by reminding the court that the case was 'but a later act of that heavy and wofull tragedie, which is commonly called the powder treason', and went on to make some general comments on the proceedings which were to come. Coke was, of course, able to fit the trial into an appropriately godly framework:

> And with this comfort I conclude the preface, that I hope in God, this dayes worke, and the judgement of so many as shal be attentive and well disposed, shall tend to the glory of Almighty God, the honour of our religion, the safety of his most excellent maiestie and his royall issue, and the securitie of the whole common wealth.

Following this preamble, he worked at length through the charges against Garnett, and managed to make a case that Garnett was indeed guilty of treason proper. He was convicted, and subjected to hanging, drawing and quartering in St Paul's courtyard on 3 May. According to at least some accounts, this was one occasion when public execution as a demonstration of state power backfired. Garnett's conduct so impressed the crowd that they rushed forward to pull on his legs as he hanged, killing him outright and thus saving him from being butchered while alive. There was also, apparently, little enthusiasm from the crowd when the executioner held the Jesuit's severed head up for inspection.

Hanging, drawing and quartering of traitors, and the ceremonies which accompanied these processes, were not new in 1605. What was new was a piece of legislation which was passed shortly after Parliament reassembled on 21 January. Two days after Parliament's return, a bill was introduced into the Commons by Sir Edward Montagu, Member of Parliament for Northamptonshire. Montagu was a known Puritan, an opponent of immorality and popular recreations in his native county, and also a patron of godly clergy there: indeed, he was still recovering from a fall from royal favour incurred a few months earlier when he had given James I a petition arguing for the reinstatement of a number of recently dismissed extreme Protestant ministers. Montagu delivered a powerful speech in which he dwelt on how great a deliverance the King and the realm had just experienced, and suggested that as this deliverance was the result of God's great favour, there should be some official provision made for the perpetual commemoration of this divine intervention. The result was perhaps the least contentious piece of legislation passed by any seventeenth-century parliament, 3 James I cap. 1, 'An Act for a Public Thanksgiving to Almighty God every Year on the Fifth Day of November'. The Almighty had saved the King, Parliament, and by extension the English nation from 'an invention so inhumane, barbarous and cruel as the like was never before heard of', and accordingly it behoved the English never to forget their deliverance, which should be 'had in perpetual remembrance, that all ages to come may yield praises to his divine majesty for the same, and have in memory this joyful day of deliverance'. Thus on 5 November each year, in every parish in England, there was to be a service, at which attendance was theoretically compulsory for all the King's loyal subjects, where thanks would be given for God's deliverance of the English from Gunpowder Treason. This annual ceremony was to keep memories of the Plot alive until it was finally taken out of the Anglican prayerbook in 1859, two and a half centuries later.

This legislation was accompanied by laws enacting harsher anti-Catholic measures, involving stricter punishments against Catholics and imposing further constraints on their civil liberties. Yet, unexpectedly, there was no universal crackdown on the King's Catholic subjects. Persecution intensified in some areas, but, as so often in the previous reign, this was essentially the product of local initiatives by enthusiastic Protestant officials. The first sermon preached on the theme of the Plot is instructive. William Barlow, Bishop of Rochester and a man who had already proved his worth on such occasions, delivered a sermon at Paul's Cross in St Paul's Cathedral churchyard on 10 November, the first Sunday after the discovery of the Plot. Paul's Cross was an important venue for preachers, and was in particular a place where sermons would be delivered providing Londoners with the official take on recent political developments. Barlow's sermon was strangely muted. Much biblical learning was deployed, but only half the sermon focused on the Plot itself. Even then, there was no encouragement of kneejerk anti-Catholicism. That the Plot was dreadful, and the conspirators Catholic, could not be denied. But Barlow was controlled in his comments, and at the end of his performance pointed out that extreme Protestants, notably John Knox and George Buchanan in Scotland a generation earlier, along with their English admirers, had posed as great a threat to divine-right monarchy as had the recent Gunpowder plotters. Even in the wake of this most disturbing of conspiracies, the authorities were still trying to encourage a middle line between Catholic and Protestant extremism.

The same theme ran through the speech delivered by James to Parliament on 9 November 1605 in the immediate aftermath of the discovery of the plot. James portrayed

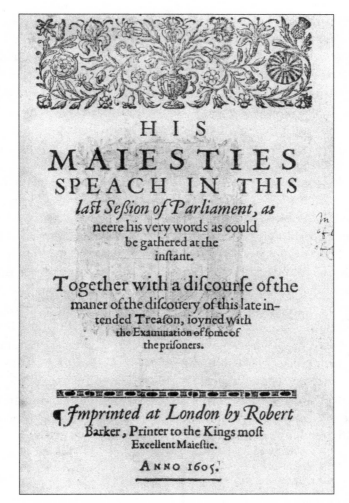

13. The printed version of King James's speech to Parliament in the immediate aftermath of the plot. This was published together with a narrative of the government version of the history of the plot, the deposition given by Guy Fawkes after torture, and the lengthy confession of Thomas Winter. Known as the King's Book, it played an important part in forming contemporary opinion about the conspiracy.

the conspiracy as terrible, and stressed the importance of divine intervention in thwarting it (he also managed a timely plug for divine right monarchy), but the overall tone was statesmanlike and restrained. There was certainly no rabid anti-Catholicism. James drew a distinction between the 'many honest men, seduced with some errors of popery, [who] may yet remaine good and faithfull subiects', and those who 'trewly know and beleeve the whole grounds' of Catholicism who could never be 'either good Christians, or faithfull subiects'. Moreover, having negotiated peace with Spain in the previous year, James was anxious to downplay the involvement of Catholic powers in the Plot. 'And for the part of forraine princes and states', he declared himself able to 'acquit them, and their ministers of their knowledge and consent to any such villanie'. Despite the enormity of this Catholic plot, the King and his advisers, once they had convinced themselves that the plotters had been apprehended, that there was no chance of a general Catholic rising, and that foreign Catholic powers were not involved, were anxious not to destabilise their diplomatic position with those Catholic powers, or further destabilise relations with the religious minority within their midst. In this, James and his ministers showed more restraint than many modern regimes faced with similar problems.

MULTIPLE MEANINGS

The twentieth century has accustomed us to the concept of the cultural revolution, of the desire of newly imposed and radical political systems to sweep away all vestiges and values of previous regimes, to construct a society founded on new and purer values and in the process to construct the new and purer human beings appropriate to such a society. At least some Protestants in late sixteenth- and seventeenth-century England regarded a cultural revolution of this type as desirable, while more moderate English Protestants envisaged the Reformation as a cultural process in which the population would be brought to higher standards of godliness. One of the elements in this process was the construction of a new calendar, in which the Saints' Days and Holy Days of the pre-Reformation Catholic Church would be replaced by something new. David Cressy, in an important study, has argued that the development of such a calendar was vital in the construction of an English Protestant consciousness:

> Under Elizabeth and the early Stuarts the English developed a relationship to time – current time within the cycle of the year, and historical time with reference to the past – that set them apart from the rest of early modern Europe. In many ways the calendar of seventeenth-century England had less in common with Renaissance France or Spain, and more with twentieth-century America or Australia. It was based on, and gave expression to, a mythic and patriotic sense of national identity. Though founded on Christianity, purged of the excesses of late medieval Catholicism, the guiding landmarks were taken from recent incidents in English history. The calendar became an important instrument for declaring and disseminating a distinctively Protestant national culture.

As the seventeenth century progressed, the Fifth was to assume and retain a central importance in this process, even though exactly what was being celebrated on the Fifth changed over time. In January 1606 King, Parliament and English Protestants were united in their sense of deliverance from Gunpowder Treason. As the political and religious conflicts of Stuart England unfolded, the message which the Fifth conveyed altered as the consensus of January 1606 came unravelled.

When the statute was passed declaring that deliverance from Gunpowder Treason should be remembered annually in perpetuity, there were already a number of other important days in the Jacobean calendar. There was 24 March, the date of James's accession as King of England, 19 June, his birthday, 25 July, the date of his coronation, and 5 August, a day of remembrance for the King's escape from the Earl of Gowrie's plot against him. In addition, although officially replaced by the dates of celebration for the new King, there was 17 November, Queen Elizabeth I's Accession Day, which was remembered by the population at large in James's reign, and which was to be mobilised at moments of crisis for the Protestant cause later in the seventeenth century.

But from the start the Fifth of November enjoyed a special significance. Among the most widely celebrated of the pre-Reformation Holy Days was 1 November, All Saints' Day, which in some places was celebrated in conjunction with All Souls' Day on 2 November. All Saints' Day in particular was very important to late medieval English Catholicism, an occasion when in many places extra candles and torches were provided to illuminate the parish church, frequently being carried there in procession. In many parishes prayers were said and bells were rung for the dead, sometimes over a period of several hours, while the royal court and many town councils observed an elaborate ceremonial. Protestantism changed all that. The reformers rejected the doctrine of purgatory, the notion that those dying in a state of grace, but not entirely purified of sin, had to rid themselves of any sinful vestiges by spending time in an intermediary place between earth and heaven. This had obvious overtones for All Saints' Day, with its praying and tolling of bells for the dead. The reformers were also hostile to Catholic ideas on the power of saints, and the notion that saints might be prayed to either individually or collectively to aid the Christian believer. The ceremonials therefore had to be purged, although it seems that persuading the population at large of this point was a lengthy struggle, probably not completed until the 1580s. An unequivocally Protestant celebration on 5 November therefore provided a handy replacement for what was now regarded as a redundant Catholic holy day, and also filled All Saints' Day's role as a festival marking the onset of winter, with celebratory bonfires defying the November darkness just as the holy candles had done. In modern parlance, Bonfire Night had replaced Hallowe'en.

Moreover, 5 November's status in the developing Protestant calendar was assured by the contemporary interpretation of the survival of English Protestantism which emphasised the importance of divine providence. All Christians, of course, believed in divine providence, the notion that God intervened personally in human affairs, sometimes in mysterious and unexpected ways, to forward his grand plan for the human race. But by the early seventeenth century it was accepted by many Englishmen that God had demonstrated special providences to the English (the Reformation itself, the early death of Mary, the long reign of the Protestant heroine Elizabeth, the defeat of the Armada), to which the great deliverance of the uncovering of the Gunpowder Plot could be added. Early in his speech to Parliament of 9 November 1605 James reminded his listeners that thanks were owed to God 'for the great and miraculous delivery he hath at this time granted to me, and to you all, and consequently to the whole body of this estate', and later noted 'the wonderful providence of God' that Guy Fawkes was taken 'having his firework for kindling ready in his pocket'. William Barlow, preaching at Paul's Cross on the following day, also dwelt on these themes, and ended by urging his audience to join him in thanking God 'for his wonderfull mercie, in preserving us from this terrible blow (as they called it) from this desperate, dreadfull and damnable attempt'. The same themes of divine deliverance and divine providence were touched upon in Sir Edward Montagu's speech introducing his bill to Parliament, and Sir Edward Coke in his speech at the trial of the conspirators.

This theme of divine providence, of the unfolding of the Almighty's scheme in national and world events, was of massive importance in seventeenth-century England. As the historian Alexandra Walsham has put it:

> Providentialism was not a marginal feature of the religious culture of early modern England, but part of the mainstream, a cluster of presuppositions which enjoyed near universal acceptance. It was a set of ideological spectacles through which individuals of all social levels and from all positions on the confessional spectrum were apt to view their universe, an invisible prism which helped them to focus the refractory meanings of both petty and perplexing events ... it was also an ingrained parochial response to chaos and crisis, a practical source of consolation in a hazardous and inhospitable environment, and

an idea which exercised practical, emotional, and imaginative influence upon those who subscribed to it.

It is easy to see how England's deliverance from the horrors of Gunpowder Treason might be fitted into this ideological and theological framework. Providentialism helped ensure the survival of the Fifth as a distinct and important festival for a century and a half after 1605.

We do not know very much about how the Fifth was remembered in the decades immediately following the Plot, although scattered evidence suggests that celebrations of some sort were widespread. Churchwarden's accounts show that 5 November was commemorated with bonfires (a traditional method of celebrating) and bells in all parts of England, a number of 5 November sermons survive, while in some cities at least the day became an occasion for civic ceremonial. At such geographically distant places as Carlisle, Norwich, Nottingham and Canterbury corporations provided music and artillery salutes, and mayors, aldermen and other civic dignitaries would process to church in their robes of office. Hence on 5 November 1607 Canterbury celebrated the day, appropriately, by igniting 106lb of gunpowder and 14lb of match, and in 1610 celebrations included a dinner for the aldermen and city officers and their wives, wine, music from the town waits and other musicians, more gunpowder explosions, and a parade by the town militia. What remains elusive is how the day was kept by the mass of the population. A clue comes from Puritan-controlled Dorchester. There 5 November was commemorated officially with a sermon, the ringing of the church bells, and bonfires and fireworks, these latter becoming a regular part of royal and civic celebrations in England and other parts of Europe from the mid-sixteenth century onwards. But a sign of less seemly celebrations came on 5 November 1632, when Dorchester's constables arrested some apprentices who had celebrated God's mercy to the elect English nation by sinking four 'double jugs' of beer at the Antelope inn.

One message which got through to respectable aldermen and drunken apprentices alike was an anti-Catholic one. Thus Thomas Taylor, preaching one of five 5 November sermons which were to be printed collectively under the title of *A Mappe of Rome*, could in 1612 inform his listeners that:

> If wee looke at the generality of his cruelty, it hath beene almost without bounds, or banks: what country in all the world hath the papists set foote into, but they have left behind them the steps, impressions, and monuments of their tyrannie ... there is never a corner of Europe, which these idolators have not washed with streames of the blood of martyrs, as history sheweth. If wee consider the multitudes of men, women, and children, on whom this crueltie hath fed, it will appeare to be most mercillesse.

Anti-Catholicism, and memories of the Plot more generally, were kept alive during James I's reign in media other than sermons. A number of popular accounts of the Plot were printed, among them John Rhodes's *A Brief Summe of the Treason intended against the King & State*, a work, as its subtitle put it, which was 'fit to instruct the simple and ignorant heerein: that they be not seduced any longer by papists', and a Latin verse narrative by the physician Francis Herring. This was originally published in 1605 under the title *Pietas Pontifica*, and was later to achieve popularity in English translations. The first of these, entitled *Popish Piety*, came in 1610 and ran to 113 stanzas, while the work was published again in 1617 as *Mischeefes Mysterie: or, Treasons Master-peece*. To these publications could be added numerous prints, among the first of them Richard Smith's *The Powder Treason, Propounded, by Sathan. Approved by Antichrist. Enterprised, by Papists. Practized by Traitors*, an ornate work whose title leaves no doubt as to its slant. And there are occasional references to the Plot's importance in the broader popular culture. Leatherhead, a character in Ben Jonson's *Bartholemew Fair*, a satirical comedy of 1614, tells how the most popular of the puppet shows he produces is '*The Gunpowder Plot*, there was a get-penny! I have presented that to an eighteen, or twentypence audience nine times in an afternoon', adding 'your home-born projects prove ever the best, they are so easy and familiar'.

James I died peacefully in 1625, to be succeeded by his son Charles. The political climate changed, and that political consensus which had been so powerful in early 1606 when Parliament passed the statute setting up a day of annual remembrance began to crumble. The process, indeed, began even before King James's death, when Prince Charles and the Duke of Buckingham, to the despair of an Hispanophobic and anti-Catholic public opinion, went to Spain in 1623 in hopes of engineering a marriage between Charles and the Infanta of Spain. The marriage plans failed, and for a few years the date of Charles's return, 7 October, became another day which was celebrated with bonfires and bells. But in 1625 Charles married another Catholic princess, Henrietta Maria of France. Public disapprobation towards the marriage took on a new edge in many places, and for the first time we have reports of effigies of the Pope and the devil (but not, be it noted, of Guy Fawkes) being burned on 5 November bonfires, much to Henrietta Maria's distress.

Between 1629 and 1640 Charles ruled without Parliament, and in this period of Personal Rule 5 November became yet more politicised. The King was not only ruling without Parliament, but he was also married to a Catholic, and he seemed to be supporting Arminianism, a diluted form of Protestantism which many of the God-fearing English regarded as the thin end of the popish wedge. A number of godly preachers used their 5 November sermons as an occasion for denouncing the current religious situation. Most notably, in 1636 two politically charged 5 November sermons led to the preacher Henry Burton being hauled before the Star Chamber, and having part of his ears cut off on the pillory, being fined £5,000, and being sentenced to life imprisonment. By this time the English church, under the leadership of Charles's trusted Arminian Archbishop of Canterbury, William Laud, was trying to establish the 5 November commemorations as occasions when all, and not just popish, sedition should be denigrated. And in 1637 Laud's chaplain, Samuel Baker, is supposed to have justified his refusal to license a reissue of an English translation of Francis Herring's poetical and heavily anti-Catholic narrative of the Plot by declaring that 'we were not so angry with the papists now, as we were about 20 yeares since, and that there was no need of any such bookes to exasperate them, there being now an endeavour to winne them to us by fairnesse and mildnesse'. One suspects that this view was not widely shared among most of England's politically and religiously aware population.

It is also ironic that Samuel Baker should have voiced that sentiment in 1637. In that year a disastrously maladroit royal religious policy north of the border prompted a pro-Calvinist rebellion in Scotland which set in motion a train of events that resulted in the outbreak of civil warfare in England in 1642. In 1640, in the face of mounting opposition, Charles I was forced to call Parliament for the first time since 1629. The aptly named Short Parliament met briefly in the spring of 1640, was dissolved, and was followed by the Long Parliament. This met on 3 November 1640, and within two days was, in a massively politically charged atmosphere, listening to sermons retelling the story of Gunpowder Treason and re-emphasising its place in English providentialist history. A year later, with anti-Catholicism honed by the breaking news of a rising among the Catholic Irish, Cornelius Burges preached a 5 November sermon to the House of Commons. Burges treated his audience to what were by now the familiar components of 5 November sermons: a reminder of God's providence in saving the English from the conspiracy, an overview of Catholic perfidy which stretched back chronologically to the reign of Mary Tudor and geographically to the Spanish Inquisition, and a short narrative of the Plot which identified Henry Garnett and his fellow Jesuits as the prime movers. But Burges also had a new angle adjusted perfectly to current circumstances. God's deliverances, he informed his audience, many of whom, he noted, had not been born in 1605, were ongoing, and were now manifest in the very calling of the Long Parliament:

> That great deliverance we now celebrate, was not as a dead bush to stop a present gap only, nor a mercy expiring with that houre and occasion; but, intended for a living, lasting, breeding mercy that hath been very fertile ever since. It was an in-let to further favours, and in earnest of many more blessings: for which, I appeal to your own experience who have duely observed God's dealing with

you ... This very parliament speaks out this truth to all the world.

As David Cressy has put it, 'That the Gunpowder Plot was not a remote historical event, but rather part of a continuing pattern of danger and deliverance, was particularly clear to the generation of the 1640s.' And as the Civil Wars progressed, the Fifth, despite the attempts of some royalist writers, was firmly captured by the Parliamentarians. Indeed, one of the most lengthy descriptions we have of a seventeenth-century firework display comes from 5 November 1647, when a display for the Lords and Commons of Parliament and the London militia, 'in commemoration of God's great mercy in delivering this kingdom from the hellish plots of papists', was laid on in Lincoln's Inn Fields. Details of this display not only show how elaborate 5 November displays might be, but also give us an impression of how sophisticated fireworks had become by this date.

The display included fireballs burning in the water, to symbolise the papists' conjuration with infernal spirits. Fireboxes, like meteors, each sent out many rockets, intimating popish spirits coming from below to act their treasonous plots against England's King and Parliament (Charles I, it will be remembered, had not been executed at this point). There was Fawkes with his dark lantern, Pluto with a fiery club representing popery, and Hercules with his fiery club. Other fireworks, each invested with a special symbolism in the great theme of the Catholic threat and its defeat, included a firewheel, sky-rockets, balloons breaking in the air with many streams of fire, 'chambers of light' demonstrating England's willingness to cherish the light of the gospel, and fireboxes among the spectators, warning them to take heed for the future and be watchful against enemies. The performance, which probably owed more than a little to pre-war royal court masques, was accompanied, as ever, by bonfires and bells.

Less spectacularly, the traditional forms of commemoration continued in the 1640s and 1650s. Gunpowder Treason sermons continued to be rooted in remembrance of 1605 and a rabid anti-Catholicism, but they also provided preachers with an opportunity to fit more recent events into the traditional providentialist mould. Certainly in these two decades there were enough uncertainties and crises to encourage the conjuring up of a reassuring providentialist history through 5 November sermons. This history could also be invoked by such publications as Samuel Clarke's *England's Remembrancer* of 1657, which invoked memories of those two 'never to be forgotten deliverances', the defeat of the Spanish Armada and the discovery of the Gunpowder Plot. And after the triumphant and victorious parliamentarian regime banned such Christian festivals as Christmas, Whitsun and Easter, the Fifth became one of the few officially approved dates on which the population as a whole could enjoy itself. Interestingly, there are some reports of private bonfires and the throwing of squibs and crackers rather than official celebrations.

All this changed with the Restoration of 1660. The Fifth was recaptured by the royalists, and 5 November sermons now argued that the great providence of the return of Charles Stuart in May 1660 was a deliverance on a par with the frustrating of Gunpowder Treason. Celebrations continued on a popular level. Samuel Pepys has left us an impression of how the day was commemorated in London. On 5 November 1660 he noted: 'The 5 of November is observed exceeding

well in the City; and at night great bonefires and fireworks.'
On the same date in the following year he recording going to
the Dolphin tavern with his brother Tom and another man,
where they 'sate late and drank much, seeing the boys in
the street fling their crackers – the day being keeped all the
day very strictly in the city'. On 5 November 1664 Pepys
went with his wife to see a production of *Macbeth* ('a pretty
good play') and on their return their coach was 'forced to go
round by London-wall home because of the bonefires – the
day being mightily observed in the city'. Pepys, therefore,
evokes an impression of a day of celebration which was
widely observed in London, with bonfires and fireworks.
In 1666, however, the year of the Great Fire of London, the
celebrations, as might be expected, were muted, while the
English, mistakenly, thought that they had another atrocity
they could attribute to the Catholics. On 5 November of that
year Pepys wrote:

> I home by coach, but met not one bonefire through the
> whole town in going round by the wall; which is strange,
> and speaks the melancholy disposition of the city at
> present, while never more was said of and feared of and
> done against the Papists than just at this time.

Blaming the Catholics for the Great Fire of London helped
revive old fears, and it was no accident that their alleged
part in the Great Fire should be inscribed on the Monument,
that 202-foot column which was raised to commemorate the
conflagration. But within a few years anti-Catholicism was
to escalate to new heights, and the Fifth was to attain a new
and more visible status as an overtly political occasion.

THE CATHOLIC THREAT RENEWED

The restoration of Charles II and the *status quo ante bellum* in May 1660 was a source of profound relief to most English men and women. But the feeling of relief and perhaps euphoria felt by many could not hide the fact that the old political tensions which had been at play before the Civil Wars broke out had not gone away. Few were prepared to admit it, and fewer still were happy about it, but the intertwined political and religious tensions of the previous twenty or thirty years were still bubbling under the surface. What brought them into the open was a religious issue of profound importance. Internationally, English fear of popery was heightened by the ambitions of Louis XIV, King of France, who was apparently intending to turn his country into a Catholic superpower on a par with Philip II's Spain of a century before. At home, Charles II and his Queen were unable to produce an heir, which left the succession open to Charles's younger brother, James, Duke of York. James had converted to Catholicism in 1672, and made this public when he refused to take the Anglican sacrament in the following year. In 1673 he married a Catholic princess, Mary of Modena. The reaction of at least one country clergyman was immediate. Ralph Josselin, vicar of Earls Colne in Essex, noted in his diary for 5 November 1673, 'preacht from ps.107.2. gods deliverance a hope to us he will deliver against the feares of popery at present in England. The duke marrying Modena's daughter.' In 1675 he included 'a narrative of the plot' in his 5 November sermon, while on 5 November 1678 he recorded his desire 'to keep it a day of holy rejoycing. If the plot now discovered had taken wee had not been owners of mercy this day.'

The newly discovered plot Josselin referred to had originated in September 1678, when Titus Oates and Israel Tonge laid before a London magistrate a set of forty-three articles purporting to reveal a Jesuit plot to assassinate Charles II, leaving the way open for James to take the throne and set up a Jesuit-directed government with the aid of a French invasion of Ireland. This 'Popish Plot' was a complete fabrication, but its reality was widely accepted, and tensions were heightened further when the magistrate who heard the original allegations, Sir Edmund Berry Godfrey, was murdered. The identity of Godfrey's killer or killers has never been established, and we can only speculate if he was killed by Catholics, by Oates or his associates to fan anti-Catholic feeling, or if the killing was unrelated to the religious politics of the period. But most contemporaries subscribed to the first of these possibilities, and anti-Catholic feeling rose yet higher. The Popish Plot assumed serious constitutional overtones, as Parliament on three occasions between 1679 and 1681 passed bills excluding James from the succession, their efforts being frustrated on each occasion by Charles using his prerogative to close Parliament. The Exclusion Crisis generated the precursors of modern political parties, with the Whigs, headed by the Earl of Shaftesbury, avidly supporting exclusion, and the Tories supporting royal policy. Many feared a revival of civil warfare, and there was general alarm at the way in which Shaftesbury's mobilization of popular support brought politics into the streets much as had happened in 1640–42. One of the actions of those taking to the streets to demonstrate for exclusion was the mobilization of the Fifth of November for their cause.

The tone was set, even before the Exclusion Crisis, on 5 November 1673 in reaction to James Duke of York's public declaration of his Catholicism. The events of that day in London are described by a contemporary pamphlet, *The*

Burning of the Whore of Babylon, as it was acted, with great Applause, in the Poultry, London, on Wednesday Night (being the 5th of November) at Six of the Clock. On that day, according to this account, 'the bells were up very early … and rang so loud, as if they had prefaced in a jubilee', while by nightfall 'you might have seen the broad streets of London so thick with bonfires, as if they had been but one hearth, and the fire-works flying in such numbers, that the serpents flew like bees through the air'. This was a more intense version of the city's normal celebrations, such as Pepys had noted. But this time London's apprentices were adding something new to the celebrations. They had made 'a large effigie of the Whore of Babylon', in fact a figure of the Pope, which had

> all the whorish ornaments, having a cross and two keys in his hand; I know not if they were the keys of the cellar that Guy Faux had, but I suppose they might belong to Purgatory, because the Pope formerly kept one, and Donna Olympia the other; he had a string of beads in his hand … he gorgeously appear'd with the Triple Crown on his head, and holding a placate in his hand, extended to the people, proclaiming general pardons; but I saw none very forward to accept them.

This figure was carried to the Poultry Market Place 'as the traitors heads are upon the bridge, fixed upon a pole', in a procession of about 1,000 people, about 100 of whom were carrying torches. A rope was strung across Poultry Street from two garret windows, and the effigy was suspended there in front of a bonfire for about two hours, with members of the crowd taking pot-shots at it with pistols and fowling pieces. The figure was eventually destroyed by having a barrel full of 'small fuel & combustable stuff' burnt underneath it, after which 'having filled themselves with good liquor, and gratified their own humours, every man and boy went to his own home, and so the play ended'.

This event set the tone for the celebration of the Fifth over the next few years. Thus in 1679, with the Exclusion Crisis at its height, it was noted that 'the 5th at night, being gunpowder treason, there were many bonfires and burning of popes as has ever been seen on the like occasion'. But the Fifth was being joined by another Protestant celebration. The 17 November, Queen Elizabeth's Accession Day, had, as we have noted, been commemorated spasmodically earlier in the seventeenth century. In the heightened mood of anti-Catholicism, celebration of this Protestant heroine, like remembrance of Gunpowder Treason, acquired a new urgency. In 1677 Elizabeth's Accession Day had been marked by elaborate celebrations in London. Charles Hatton wrote to his brother:

> Last Saturday the coronation of Queen Elizabeth was solemnized in the city with mighty bonfires and the burning of a most costly pope, carried by four persons in divers habits, and the effigies of two devils whispering in his ears, his belly filled with live cats who squalled most hideously as soon as they felt the fire; the common saying all the while was the language of the pope and the devil in a dialogue betwixt them. A tirce [42 gallons] was set out before the Temple gate for the common people. Mr Langthorne saith he is very confident the pageantry cost forty pounds.

Similarly elaborate celebrations took place on the Fifth during

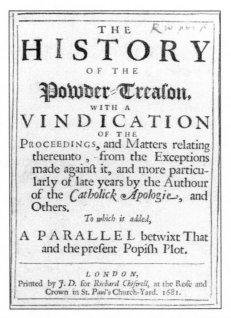

14. The History of the Powder-Treason, *by John Williams, Bishop of Chichester. As the subtitle suggests, the history of the Gunpowder Plot was a powerful resource to draw upon when rekindling anti-Catholic fears at the time of the Popish Plot and Exclusion Crisis in the years around 1680. At that time a number of new works on the Gunpowder Plot and other Catholic acts of aggression and atrocities were published, and old ones reprinted.*

the late 1670s. But by 1681 the tide was flowing against exclusion, and on at least one occasion the Tories were able to highjack the Fifth for their own purposes. At Westminster School, presumably a Tory stronghold, on 5 November 1681 schoolboys burnt an effigy of 'Jack Presbyter'.

The early 1680s were to see the waning of exclusion as an organised political movement, but the Fifth retained its significance in popular politico-religious sentiments. In 1682,

5 November fell on a Sunday, so the official celebrations were postponed until the following day. But 5 November 1682 was to witness severe public disorder in London. Crowds roamed the streets, attacking Tories and the houses of known Tory adherents, and shouting their support for the Duke of Monmouth, Charles II's illegitimate son and a Protestant hero. The mob was eventually contained by the City militia, although the commanding officer refused to obey the Lord Mayor's instructions to open fire on them. A number of ringleaders were subsequently pilloried, but on this occasion the public punishment of political offenders turned against the authorities. The offenders

> were brought in coaches to the places where they stood in the pillory, at each of which had assembled a numerous company of the rabble, amongst them several sturdy fellows, who appeared more than ordinarily diligent to encourage the criminals and threatened everyone that did but speak against them, saying they would be for a Monmouth and would burn the pope for all this. They drank healths with huzzas with the wine sent them and impudently made a mock of their punishment.

In 1683 the authorities acted to forestall any repetition of the public disorders of the previous year. A proclamation banning bonfires and fireworks was published, and apparently enforced successfully, while in 1684 Charles II was to congratulate the Lord Mayor of London for keeping the Fifth free of disorders.

But in the following year, 1685, the unthinkable happened: James succeeded Charles on his brother's death, and England had a Catholic king. John Evelyn the diarist, a regular hearer of 5 November sermons, recorded that he was prevented from attending the 5 November service in that year by a bad cold, 'to my greate sorrow, it being the first Gunpowder Conspiracy Anniversary that had ben kept now these 80 yeares, under a Prince of the Roman religion: Bonfires forbidden &c: what does this portend?' What it portended for the Fifth, as Evelyn noted, was a banning of bonfires and other forms of celebrations, although the sermons continued (Evelyn recorded attending a solidly anti-Catholic one the following year). What it portended for the English political nation was rather more serious. Noblemen, gentry, Oxford dons, town corporations, and bishops all had their privileges eroded, Catholics and Dissenters received advancement, and James enlarged his army, a force which, it was feared, could all too easily be turned against his Protestant subjects. Such fears were deepened by events in France. The year 1685 also witnessed the revocation by Louis XIV of the Edict of Nantes, which had permitted limited toleration to French Huguenots. From 1681 Louis had been harassing his Protestant subjects by billeting soldiers, especially dragoons, light cavalrymen with a reputation for indiscipline, upon them. Reports of theft, rape and murder soon began to proliferate, causing even Louis's advisers to counsel the cautious application of the policy. But on one level the plan worked: a large number of France's 1,500,000 Huguenots converted rather than face what became known as the *dragonades*. Yet the measure, together with the revocation, added to the catalogue of Catholic atrocities, and as with the Spaniards a century earlier, tales of French anti-Protestant atrocities lost nothing in the telling. Moreover, some 400,000 Huguenots managed to escape from France, bringing their skills (many of them were artisans) to the Dutch Republic, Prussia and

England, where a vibrant community of Huguenot silk-weavers settled in Spitalfields in London. All of these brought their own stories of atrocity and repression to the Protestant countries in which they settled.

The English ruling class was thus placed in a quandry. In their eyes, James was attacking both their liberties and their Protestantism (the two were, of course, conceived as being inextricably interconnected) at a time when the Catholic menace was reviving on an international level. But few people were willing to risk a civil war that might lead to a return to something like the Cromwellian and Republican regimes of 1649–60, when men of property had felt themselves threatened by social upstarts and religious enthusiasts backed by the New Model Army. The solution lay in William of Orange, Stadholder of the Netherlands, the husband of James II's daughter Mary. William was a man who could, through his marriage, make a plausible claim to the throne, and who was also a strong Protestant. Feelers were put out, and a deal was struck. The English elite were to have their privileges and their religion guaranteed, with a dual monarchy to preserve the social order. In return William of Orange was allowed to mobilise England's resources in his life and death struggle against the hegemony of Louis XIV's France. In late October 1688, after a false start, he sailed for England with a fleet carrying 15,000 Dutch troops, eventually landing at Torbay in Devon.

The date of the landing was 5 November.

A DOUBLE DELIVERANCE

England now had a double deliverance from popery to celebrate on the Fifth, and the 5 November sermons of 1689

A

SERMON

Preached before the

House of Peers

IN THE

ABBEY of WESTMINSTER,

On the 5th. of *November* 1689.

BEING

GUN-POWDER TREASON-DAY,

As Likewise

The Day of his Majefties Landing

IN

ENGLAND.

By the Right Reverend Father in God *GILBERT*
Lord Bifhop of *SARVM.*

LONDON,
Printed for Ric. Chifwel at the *Rofe* and *Crown* in
St. *Pauls Church-yard.* MDCLXXXIX.

15. Title page of the 5 November sermon by Gilbert Burnet, Bishop of
Salisbury, to the House of Lords at Westminster Abbey, 1689. Such sermons
were important in showing how the story of the Gunpowder Plot was constantly adjusted to help explain changing political circumstances. And, as
is suggested here, from 1689 onwards Gunpowder Treason sermons usually
also referred to the landing of William of Orange in England on 5 November
1688. Burnet had, in fact, attached himself to William's cause while in exile
before 1688.

did not fail to make this point. They also showed how, once again, the celebration of this deliverance could be linked to ongoing political issues. One of the more upmarket Gunpowder Treason sermons of that year was delivered by Gilbert Burnet to the members of the House of Lords assembled in Westminster Abbey. Burnet was a long-time Whig supporter who, while in exile during the previous reign, had entered William of Orange's service and was rewarded with the vacant see of Salisbury immediately after his patron's landing. Following a familiar theme, he commented on England's special status in the eyes of the Almighty, claiming that 'it may be affirmed without any arrogant preferring of our nation to theirs, or any partiality for our selves, in imagining that we are God's favourite people'. In support of this contention, he rehearsed that familiar Protestant and providentialist interpretation of English history in which God gave the English the Reformation, saved that Reformation from 'the terrible but short shaking it had in Queen Mary's time', gave the English 'the long and glorious reign of Queen Elizabeth', saved them from the Armada and heaped a number of other blessings on them, including, by the late seventeenth century, 'the encrease of our trade, the many colonies we have sent into America'. But he turned the occasion to look at current problems as well as past history. Inventively, Burnet managed to assert French involvement in the Gunpowder Plot, and then turned to the more immediate threat offered by Louis XIV. 'And when I have named France,' declared Burnet, 'I have said all that is necessary to give you a compleat idea of the blackest tyranny over men's consciences, persons, and estates, that can possibly be imagined,' a land where the property, persons and beliefs of subjects were 'at the mercy of a boundless power, and of a severity that has no mixtures either of truth or goodness to govern or allay it'. Faced with such a monstrous opponent, Burnet hoped that the English 'would turn to God in good earnest'.

If the second deliverance of William III's landing meant that Gunpowder Treason lost its unique significance for 5 November, it also meant that, as in the early seventeenth century, 5 November became one of a number of competing days of celebration. The crucial issue was that 4 November was a day of specially significance for Dutch William: it was the day of his birth, in 1650, and also of his marriage to Mary Stuart, in 1677. In London at least, this double day of royal celebration threatened to eclipse the Fifth. A key source here is Narcissus Lutrell's *A Brief Historical Relation of State Affairs.* In 1689, Lutrell recorded on 4 November that 'being the birth day of his present majestie, was observed; the shops were shutt all day, and ringing of bells and bonefires at night' and 'a great ball at court'. The next day, 'being the anniversary thanksgiving for the discovery of the gunpowder plott, was kept with great rejoyceings ... and it was observed the more, being the day of his present majesties landing in England'. In 1690, Lutrell tells us

> The 4th, being his majesties birth day, was observed here very strictly, by shutting up the shops, firing the great guns at the Tower, ringing of bells, and bonefires at night; their majesties dined publickly at Whitehall, where was a great resort of nobility and gentry, and a night was a consort of musick, and a play afterwards. And the next day, being the anniversary of the gunpowder plott (being likewise the day of his maiesties landing in England) was observed with great solemnity and general rejoycing.

Other comments from the later 1690s confirm this impression that, for the court and political elite at least, the celebrations on 4 November were of greater significance, and more worthy of attention, than those on the following day.

William died in March 1702 (Mary had passed away in 1694), and although the 5 November sermons continued to celebrate the double deliverances of 1605 and 1688, it was the commemoration of Gunpowder Treason which lay at the heart of popular and civic celebrations on that day. The Fifth had survived its first century after going through several changes, and it was to continue to survive, adjusting to circumstances as it went. But what is most striking to the modern observer about the Fifth's first century is that Guy Fawkes had not yet assumed his key role in the public celebration of the Fifth. The crises of the 1670s had seen popes, devils, and prominent Catholics or Catholic sympathisers on the bonfires: but as yet effigies of York's most famous son were rarely consumed by the flames.

4

CHANGING TIMES AND THE
REINVENTION OF GUY FAWKES

THE SLOW ROAD TO CATHOLIC EMANCIPATION

Thomas Amyot, an articled clerk in Norwich, was an intelligent young man who, like so many intelligent young men of his generation, was excited by the spirit of liberty that had been unleashed by the French Revolution. On 12 November 1794 he wrote to a like-minded friend, William Pattisson, on the subject of 'stated national festivals'. Among other things, he animadverted on the Fifth:

> As to the celebration of the fifth of November; in respect of the Gunpowder Treason. I think it ought to have ceased with its century, or perhaps 50 years would have been a sufficient period for it; as the event cannot under the circumstances which have since happened be deemed of any very considerable magnitude. But I believe it does no harm; those who make a noise on the fifth of November harbour very little spleen in their hearts against the Catholics who are now so very peaceable a class of men that it would be the highest injustice to molest them and indeed our laws have lately very wisely restored many

of their former privileges ... But it so happens that the
Gunpowder Plot affords a pretext for a little noise; that
is the event which is celebrated, while the other is almost
forgotten.

Amyot was, alas, rather optimistic in his reading of the
decline in anti-Catholic feeling. But his views are interesting in demonstrating how an intelligent observer could see
changes in the celebration of Gunpowder Treason, changes
through which the traditional remembrance of a national
deliverance was being replaced by 'a pretext for a little
noise'.

At the beginning of the eighteenth century, such changes
would have been unthinkable. The Gunpowder Plot and
what it had come to mean in post-1688 English Protestant
consciousness enjoyed a profound importance. This was
demonstrated in 1709, when a 5 November sermon chal-
lenging the Fifth's conventional meaning provoked a political crisis. This year fell in a period of intense party conflict
between Whigs and Tories, and hence between low-church
and high-church attitudes, with the Tories constantly taunt-
ing the Whigs as the inheritors of that extreme Puritanism
which, on the Tory interpretation, lay behind the execution
of Charles I. On 5 November of that year, Henry Sacheverell,
a high-church clergyman, preached a sermon before an
important audience at St Paul's Cathedral. This equated the
Gunpowder conspirators with the men who had killed King
Charles, and declared that the 1688 Revolution constituted
an act of unjustifiable rebellion. Sacheverell dismissed the
Catholic threat in a few introductory pages, and then spent
about an hour and a half preaching against the inequities of
sectaries and schismatics. The Whig government could not

ignore this challenge, and Sacheverell was impeached by the House of Lords for his sermon and found guilty. The government was anxious to treat the errant clergyman harshly, but Queen Anne intervened on his behalf and he was merely banned from preaching for three years. During his trial there was a severe escalation of the Whig–Tory conflict, manifested among other things by the sacking and burning of dissenting chapels by high-church mobs. The sermon reputedly sold 100,000 copies.

The Sacheverell affair is instructive in demonstrating how the Fifth could still be a politically contested date, but in fact by the early eighteenth century most 5 November sermons were much more conventional. The message delivered on that day, well into the nineteenth century, was a clear one: the papists had attempted to blow up Parliament in 1605; this was just one of a series of blows they had contemplated or delivered against Protestantism in general and English Protestantism in particular; there was every expectation that they would attempt something equally dastardly in the future; and only vigilance and trust in a God who had showed his special providence for the English would ensure future safety. And, of course, as almost every preacher of a Gunpowder Treason sermon reminded his listeners, 5 November was doubly auspicious in the English Protestant calendar, marking as it did William of Orange's landing at Torbay and the consequent saving of the English from the imposition of Catholic tyranny by James II.

So throughout the early eighteenth century the deliverances of 1605 and 1688 continued to be mobilised to demonstrate both God's special favouring of the English and the ongoing popish threat against them. The sermons delivered on 5 November were occasions to utilise past experience to sharpen perceptions of, and inform comment upon, the unfolding series of political events which followed the Glorious Revolution. As we have noted, Louis XIV of France was, by 1688, providing English propagandists with a Catholic tyrant as odious as Philip II of Spain had been, and one of the consequences of the arrival of William of Orange on the English throne was the mobilisation of English resources against French hegemony in Europe. William Dawes, a future Archbishop of York, preaching before the University of Cambridge on the centenary of the Plot, 5 November 1705, could add to the conventional warning of the need to be vigilant against the machinations of popery an exhortation to support the war effort against Louis, noting a special duty 'to pay our taxes willingly and freely'. By 1705, of course, William III was dead, having been succeeded by Anne in 1703, and her accession prompted further patriotic asides in Fifth of November sermons. Philip Stubs (or Stubbs), preaching at St Paul's Cathedral before the Lord Mayor and Court of Aldermen of London, referred to her as 'a queen, whose heart is entirely Protestant as well as English', and ended his sermon with two pages of praise for her. In 1721 the smooth accession of the Protestant, if German, House of Hanover to the British throne aroused similar thanks that the English royal line was Protestant, while the failure of the Jacobite rebellions of 1715 and 1745 gave further evidence of both Catholic perfidy and God's willingness to help the English defeat it. These 5 November sermons show us one way in which the ideology of the post-1688 constitution was brought to the population at large. They also demonstrate the continued importance of the perpetuation of a providentialist history in which past Catholic threats loomed large.

Yet these sermons also provide indications that the fear

of Catholics, *all* Catholics, was slowly receding, while by the mid-eighteenth century at least some preachers were adopting a moderate tone. On 5 November 1753 John Garnett, Bishop of Ferns and Leighlin, preached a sermon in Christ Church, Dublin, to commemorate, conventionally enough, 'the anniversary of the Gunpowder-Plot and of the happy arrival of King William III'. Anti-Catholicism was largely absent from this sermon, and the reign of James II, while mentioned, was not dwelt upon. Garnett was concerned not with raking over past history, but rather with celebrating the political and indeed economic status quo in the realms of George III. He exhorted his audience to pray for the safety of kings, since

> thus we may be enabled, under the safe shelter of government, to lead a quiet, and peaceable life, in all godliness and honesty, i.e. through the just and prudent administration of it, we may be in a capacity of receiving the natural, and genuine fruits of good government, peace and good order; the preservation of our most holy religion; and the security of our property, by the support, and enforcement of moral honesty.

Garnett also noted 'the florishing [sic] state of our commerce', 'the improvement of our manufactures, to that degree of exquisiteness, and perfection, which bespeaks both an ingenious, and industrious people', 'the cultivation of the liberal arts and sciences ... and indeed for all the advantages, which tend either to the conveniency, or the ornament of social life'. These were the measured and polished tones of the Enlightenment, rather than the jagged accents of seventeenth-century religious controversy. Garnett expressed the hope that 'the Christian world at length will be right rid of crusades and pilgrimages, those quixoticisms in religious chivalry', and that holy war, 'that pious solecism in holy-church politicks', should 'be now no more'.

From the mid-eighteenth century matters gradually improved for England's Catholics. It became less acceptable to express rabidly anti-Catholic views in polite society. After about 1760 most justices of the peace seem to have quietly discontinued the prosecution of recusants. In 1778 and 1791 there were Catholic Relief Acts, the first of these, among other things, allowing Catholics to serve in the British army and legally purchase and inherit land, the second permitting the building of Catholic chapels and churches and allowing Catholics to enter the legal profession. Moreover, at the same time as rabid anti-Catholicism was becoming less acceptable in refined society, so too was traditional providentialist Protestantism. Among the educated it was supplanted by the more measured, rational Christianity of the Enlightenment.

Yet there was still considerable anti-Catholicism among the population at large, and indeed among many of their social superiors. The first Catholic Relief Act prompted the formation of the Protestant Association, presided over from late 1779 by the mentally unstable Lord George Gordon. An attempt by the Association to petition Parliament against the Act on 2 June 1780 sparked off a week of rioting in London, known to posterity as the Gordon Riots, which began with attacks on the houses of prominent Catholics and ended with assaults by the drink-fuelled mob on Newgate prison and the Bank of England. This was the worst disorder experienced in eighteenth-century London, with over 200 rioters shot down by the military and a further twenty-

16. James Gillray's depiction of a Gordon Rioter, 1780. One of the consequences of the Gordon Riots, the most serious and destructive outbreak of popular violence in eighteenth-century London, was to leave many respectable observers convinced of the connection between anti-Catholicism and mob violence. The values which underlay Gillray's print would have been shared by many respectable members of small-town society faced by 5 November rioters in the nineteenth century.

five subsequently executed. Yet the second Act caused little comment and not much opposition. Lord George Gordon was by then incarcerated in Newgate prison, where he had been imprisoned for libel. He was to die there in 1793, having meanwhile converted to Judaism, become a keen supporter of the French Revolution, and learnt how to play the bagpipes. Perhaps the most important consequence of the riots named after him was that moderate opinion began to associate anti-Catholicism with mob violence.

The growing acceptance of Catholicism was given an unexpected helping hand by the French Revolution. Here was a threat to the British constitution and the British way of life which was not only decidedly non-Catholic, but also, in its early stages at least, thorough-goingly anti-Catholic. During the wars against the Revolution and Napoleon, England's Catholics remained firmly patriotic (as, indeed, most of them had during the 1745 Jacobite invasion), and many of them served in the armed forces. This was even more true of Irish Catholics, who had formed a large proportion of the personnel of the British army during the wars, while the army in Ireland, three-quarters of its rank and file Catholics, had stayed loyal in the face of the 1798 rising. Yet full Catholic emancipation, on both sides of the Irish Sea, remained a political impossibility, with governments falling over the issue in 1801 and 1807.

It was the situation in Ireland which was to bring about Catholic emancipation in England. In 1800 Britain and Ireland had been politically unified (or, more accurately, Ireland had been politically incorporated into Britain), with, in particular, Irish Members of Parliament sitting at Westminster. This union brought little obvious benefit to the Irish at large, and there was endemic civil unrest in the early nineteenth century. In 1823 Daniel O'Connell, an Irish barrister of aristocratic background, had launched the Catholic Association with the aim of overthrowing the Act of Union. The suppression of the Association two years later did nothing to defuse the situation in Ireland, while in 1828 matters reached a head when O'Connell won a by-election in County Clare. As a Catholic, he would not take the Test Act, and hence would be refused his seat in the Commons. And if he were refused his seat in the Commons, it was feared by the British establishment, civil war would break out in Ireland. Sir Robert Peel and the Duke of Wellington, both hitherto ardent opponents of Catholic emancipation, now saw it as the lesser of two evils. What had up until shortly before been regarded as an impossible political step was rushed through both houses with great speed, and the 'Act for the Relief of his Majesty's Roman Catholic Subjects' was passed on 13 April 1829. Catholics could now enjoy full civil liberties, could serve in corporations, could sit as MPs, and occupy all but a few Crown offices. The Act was passed in the face of massive opposition. King George IV was himself an opponent, Parliament received between 2,000 and 3,000 petitions, some of them signed by more than 20,000 people, against the Act, while 202 Members of Parliament and 118 peers had voted against it. But from the passing of the Act English Roman Catholics had to be regarded differently; and so did the Fifth of November.

GUNPOWDER PLOT ON THE STAGE

In the decades surrounding the turn of the eighteenth and nineteenth centuries – between the Gordon Riots and Catholic emancipation – a decisive change occurred in the celebration

17. *A print of 1818, interesting because it shows how the modern usage of 'Guy' as an appellation for a young man was already current in early nineteenth-century England ('La' bless me what a Guy,' the woman to the left is saying). Note the small boys carrying a chair to the left of the picture, similar to that in the illustration 19, and those with the empty chair in the bottom right-hand corner. One boy cries, 'Stop that runaway Guy,' and another is crying, 'Stop that Dandy Pope,' suggesting that the two figures were still to some extent interchangeable in the early nineteenth century.*

of the Fifth. This was the emergence of Guy Fawkes as the key figure in public perceptions of the Gunpowder Plot. The reasons for this are unclear: perhaps with anti-Catholicism becoming less acceptable, and with the papacy sharing Britain's hostility to revolutionary France in the 1790s, burning effigies of the Pope was no longer encouraged. Yet Guy Fawkes's arrival is evident enough. Unlike Catesby and Garnett, Fawkes was hardly ever mentioned in eighteenth-century Gunpowder Treason sermons, while his name does not appear to have figured in titles of books and tracts published before 1800. But such works began to be published in the early nineteenth century, while by that time references to effigies of Fawkes being burnt were becoming more numerous. But in these literary works Guy Fawkes became in large measure a reinvented figure. Nowhere was this more true than in the popular theatre of the period.

Plays could be used to mobilise patriotic sentiment. On 30 October 1793 a 'Prelude in One Act' entitled *Guy Fawkes, or the Fifth of November* was performed at the Royal Haymarket Theatre. This was, in fact, a romantic farce, with Fifth of November celebrations forming a background to the main plot. One of the characters was Major Knapsack, guardian of the female lead, Fanny Fitall, and a patriotic old soldier who was a firm believer in maintaining national ceremonies. When another character dismisses Knapsack's observance of the Fifth as a whim, the old soldier replies roundly, 'Whim, say you! If loyalty is a whim it is one which I am countenanced in by nearly the whole nation … And yet shall I be ridiculed in my zealous commemoration of this day of recalling to mind an event, the glorious show of royal ability and divine mercy,' and later in the play invites his critic to drink 'a health to king and constitution and a hot fire to all inflammatory bodies'. In 1793 Britain was embroiled in war with a new threat in the form of revolutionary France, and Major Knapsack's views on how and why the Fifth of November should be celebrated struck a responsive chord with those in the auditorium. *The Times* of 6 November 1793 reported that 'the loyal sentiments entrusted to Major Knapsack were highly regarded by the audience, particularly where he defends his whim for keeping Red Letter Days, by asserting that Loyalty is the whim of the whole nation'. The point was emphasised, as *The Times* noted, by having 'God Save the King' sung at the beginning and end of the performance, and by a 'transparency' deemed 'both brilliant and appropriate' depicting William III.

Such patriotic fervour was very fitting in the atmosphere of 1793. But plays produced over the next few decades demonstrated to what extent the theatre-going public was being treated to very different takes on the Gunpowder Plot. Perhaps most surprisingly, it was being used as the basis for pantomime. On 16 November 1835 a 'Comic Pantomime' entitled *Harlequin and Guy Fawkes: or the 5th of November* was performed at the Theatre Royal Covent Garden, the title alluding to how, after the Plot is discovered, Guy Fawkes changes into Harlequin and Catesby into Pantaloon, and pure pantomime begins. This piece was typical of the early nineteenth-century pantomime, a *genre* which is recognisably the forerunner of the modern British pantomime, that great peculiarity of the nation's culture. The action begins in the Palace of Discontent, with Winter Discontent plotting mischief with the assistance of various Blue Devils. Discontent decides to shatter human tranquillity by blowing up Parliament with the assistance of 'A swaggering roaring boisterous invader/ That came to England in the famed Armada/Who fears not for Reformers or hard knocks/ A man of metal true call'd Guido Fawkes.' The excruciating rhyming couplets deployed here were typical of these pantomimes, while another of their peculiarities was the constant use of what were then modern references: Guy Fawkes's indifference to 'Reformers' might bring forth knowing chuckles in a production staged only three years after the 1832 Reform Act. Another one of these farces, *Guy Fawkes: the Ugly Mug and the Couple of Spoons*, was staged in a year of mounting pressure for Parliamentary reform, 1866 (the second Reform Act was passed in 1867). This too contains topical allusions. Thus as he waits beneath the House of Lords, Guy Fawkes declares, 'So I, the demagogue of democracy/Am in the chambers of the aristocracy/To whom I bear the very deepest malice/ Except to one lovely maiden – Alice.' And in this production (another common theme of these comic variations on the tale of Gunpowder Treason), James I is played as a caricature Scotsman.

The fullest of these Gunpowder Plot pantomimes was *Guy Fawkes or a Match for a King*, staged at various points throughout the nineteenth century. On 31 October 1855 it was performed, allegedly by 'a company of amateurs', at the Theatre Royal Olympic in London. This production offered a novel twist on the Mounteagle letter. Catesby is a director of the Accidental Death Insurance Company, and as he sits smoking a pipe on the powder barrels he suddenly realises that Mounteagle is insured by the company, and writes a letter to him warning him not to attend Parliament in order to avoid having to make a large insurance payment. Guy Fawkes, 'A Spanish Dutchman kindly disposed to give Parliament a lift', makes his entry offstage in a hansom cab, and promptly gets into a row with the cabbie about the fare. Contemporary references abound: the Crimean War gets a mention, but as a source of comedy rather than patriotic fervour, as do the railway service from Waterloo station and the great Victorian historian T.B. Macaulay (in a song, Catesby wishes that Macaulay could be there to tell the story), while there is even a joke about the incomprehensibility of J.M.W. Turner's paintings. What is totally lacking is any reference to the more serious undertones of the Plot, and there is no mention of religion. The history of the Plot was, in these productions, entirely marginalised. Indeed, one of the few references to the historical resonances of the Plot, in

Guy Fawkes: the Ugly Mug and a Couple of Spoons, encouraged this state of affairs:

> When crackling faggots make the bonfire hot,
> Let prejudice with faggots be *faggot*,
> And let tar barrels with their roasting ribs,
> present the only objects for your squibs.
> Let old antipathies in crackers end,
> And polemics with fire balloons ascend.

For the writers of these pantomimes the Fifth's old role in touching an anti-Catholic and patriotic nerve was totally redundant. One is also struck by the awful pun turning on 'faggot' and 'forgot', a joke invoking the old 'Remember, remember' rhyme.

Much the same can be said of the more serious dramatic productions telling the story of Guy Fawkes and the Gunpowder Plot. For one example, let us consider *Guido Fawkes: or, the Prophetess of Ordsall Cave*. This play was performed at the Queen's Theatre, Manchester, in June 1840, its plot derived from the early episodes of the serialised version of what was to be published in the following year as William Harrison Ainsworth's *Guy Fawkes and the Gunpowder Plot*, a work full of Mancunian allusions. In this production Fawkes was portrayed as a politically motivated sympathiser with the common people's cause. At one point, watching over Elizabeth Orton, an elderly prophetess who figures prominently in the early stages of the drama, he expresses himself thus:

> Poor sufferer! Your couch is less rugged than the hearts
> of persecutors – it is thus they would bruise and trample

18. Guy Fawkes as action hero, laying the powder trail which will ignite the barrels under Westminster Palace: another illustration by George Cruikshank for Ainsworth's Guy Fawkes, or the Gunpowder Treason.

upon all who have the sin of poverty upon their souls; but I shall yet live to set my foot on many of their proud necks – the day will come, haughty masters, deceive not yourselves. Ye look upon the poor as slaves, and set up rulers over them; any law you make is but to keep them more in subjection. They are ground down to better their morals; their harmless sports cut, less they should become vicious; their hours of relaxation limit their fear they grow idle. Kind, considerate rulers are ye! But the time will assuredly dawn when the people will shake off all these galling fetters; when every man shall sit under his own roof, and none shall have power to make him fear. Hear me, ye lords of the earth, who have for your possessions too much yearly – you evil giants of England – ye who keep a city guard to feed the beggars on stones – to imprison like dogs, the poor and helpless. Hear my warning and beware! Ye are sharpening the fangs of the people; and when ye least dream it, will find their teeth buried fast and deeply in your throats! Ye are going full gallop to the devil!

This was clearly an appropriate Guy Fawkes for a radical city like Manchester.

A more conventional treatment of the Plot in a serious play came with George Macfarren's *Guy Fawkes; or, the Gunpowder Treason. An Historical Melo-Drama, in Three Acts.* Macfarren (1788–1843) was a prolific writer of plays and opera librettos, collaborating in some of his operatic works with his son George Alexander (1813–87), in his time a composer of some note. In Macfarren's play, first performed in 1822, the Gunpowder conspirators are presented as patriots whose aim is to overturn a tyrannical foreign despot and his parasitic court. The best lines on this theme are given to Sir Everard Digby:

> 'Tis certain – we are beset on every hand; the locusts of the court, like the locusts of the wilderness, eat up our goodly fruit, and poison even the root and branches … In short, without some remedy in public deeds, in private actions, in church as well as state, the land is ruined; and goodly England, so long adorned with conquering laurels, shall sink to be a crouching slave to every upstart foe … Shall the free sons of Albion stoop to despot power, bend to a coward, yield their fair honours to deck Scottish sychophants, and owe allegiance to a foreigner – No.

As might be expected, King James is portrayed as a stage Scotsman with a taste for pedantry, while Salisbury is not a very sympathetic character. Following what appears to have been a standard convention, Fawkes is represented as a Spaniard – as Catesby puts it, 'a Spaniard by birth, but whose obdurate soul and countless crimes extirpate him from his native soil, and fit him for the direst occupations'. Indeed, as Fawkes lays the powder trail under the House of Lords, he declares his intention to 'do this mighty deed as becomes a true Spaniard'. Whilst he could hardly be called a sympathetic character, Fawkes is portrayed as what could be described as an action anti-hero, a hard man of tremendous courage and resolution. Macfarren's play, which seems to have been widely republished and which also formed the basis for a child's toy theatre drama, clearly gave a very distinctive spin to the Guy Fawkes story.

Representation of Guy Fawkes and the Gunpowder Plot in nineteenth-century popular theatre demonstrates how history was being variously re-written or forgotten altogether, how the old story of the Plot was constantly being refashioned, and how Guy Fawkes, from the very beginning of the nineteenth century, had assumed a new identity as the key figure in the Plot. We can trace this in other media.

THE NEW CONSENSUS

In the comic play *Guy Fawkes or a Match for a King*, whose staging of 1855 we have already noted, Guy Fawkes, contemplating execution, comments that 'One hope is left me once all others fail/when my head's off Ainsworth shall write my tale.' The reference, immediately understandable to contemporary audiences, was to William Harrison Ainsworth, a once massively successful but now virtually forgotten author. In July 1841 Ainsworth wrote Fawkes's tale in a novel entitled *Guy Fawkes, or the Gunpowder Treason: an Historical Romance*. This 'historical romance' respected the main lines of the history of the Plot, but added numerous embellishments. Ainsworth was a native of Manchester, and added Mancunian or Lancastrian themes to many of his works. Accordingly, Guy Fawkes makes his first appearance in the novel at an execution of seminary priests at Salford, while nearby Ordsall figures prominently in the book. A key character is Humphrey Chetham, a real historical figure who founded Chetham's library and Chetham's hospital at Manchester, but who had no known connections either with Guy Fawkes or the Gunpowder Plot. Ainsworth also added a romantic dimension to the story. Chetham is madly in love with Viviana Radcliffe, daughter of the Radcliffes of Ordsall Hall, but she, a Catholic, rejects the advances of her Protestant suitor and contemplates entering a nunnery. She does, however, fall in love with Guy Fawkes, who eventually reciprocates, and the two are married by Henry Garnett – though Viviana, imprisoned for misprision of treason, dies of despair in the Tower of London shortly before Guy's execution. Another twist is that Tresham's death in the Tower is attributed to poison administered to him by Mounteagle as part of a plan by Salisbury. And as yet another twist, Mounteagle, disguised as a Catholic priest, administers the last rites to Tresham, and then takes incriminating papers from him.

As with all of Ainsworth's novels, it is the fast-moving plot which is important in *Guy Fawkes*, rather than the developments of character or philosophising over the story. The novel began, as was the custom of the day, in serial form, being published in *Bentley's Magazine* between January 1840 and November 1841, but was published as a triple-decker, complete with illustrations by George Cruikshank, three-quarters of the way through its serialisation. To Ainsworth's Edwardian biographer *Guy Fawkes* was 'one of Ainsworth's best romances; very carefully written, the original scheme laid down skillfully traced through intricate ways to its final gloomy *dénoument*, it is also the most physical of all its author's books'. Modern readers would probably not share this enthusiasm; but they would certainly be struck by the very sympathetic portrayal of Guy Fawkes. Throughout he is depicted as a loner, whose involvement with Viviana Radcliffe goes against his personal grain, but also as a man endowed with principle and courage. The courage is demonstrated at the very beginning of the book by his rescue from the River Irwell of the prophetess Elizabeth Orton. The theme recurs constantly, perhaps most memorably when Fawkes declares his decision not to use a slow match to ignite the powder barrels under the House of Lords, but rather, as Ainsworth has him say, 'I will see the deed done, and if the train fails, will hold a torch to the barrels myself.' At another point, Fawkes makes an important statement to Viviana about how he regards what he is doing:

> Man cannot read my heart, but heaven can; and the sincerity of my purpose will be recognised above. What I am about to do is for the regeneration of our holy religion; and if the welfare of that religion is dear to the Supreme Being, our cause must prosper. If the contrary, it deserves to fail, and will fail. I have ever told you that I care not what becomes of myself.

Thus, in the story of the Gunpowder Plot as told by this most popular of novelists, Guy Fawkes becomes a brave and sympathetic character, and his cause a worthy one.

This is mirrored by Ainsworth's less than approbatory treatment of England's Protestant authorities. Many of the individual Protestants in Ainsworth's novel are portrayed favourably, and Humphrey Chetham is by far the most sympathetic male character in the book. But Ainsworth is at pains to stress what he considered to be the oppressive nature of the treatment of Catholics. The tone is set in his preface, where he attributes 'the remarkable conspiracy about to be related' to 'the tyrannical measures adopted against the Roman Catholics in the early part of the reign of James the First, when the severe penal enactments against recusants were revived'. King James I receives the by then customary treatment as a coward and a pedant, while Salisbury emerges as a machiavellian statesman. If Humphrey Chetham is the most sympathetic character, Topcliffe, the avid hunter of recusants and priests, is the most unsympathetic . And there is also a harrowing description of the sufferings of Viviana Radcliffe when, after being imprisoned in the Tower, she is subjected to the torture of the gauntlets. This, a standard form of torture in 1605, was applied to the real Guy Fawkes. But Ainsworth's depiction of torture in Jacobean England goes beyond historical reality. At one point he has Guy Fawkes penned up in 'the dungeon among the rats', a pit twenty feet wide and twelve deep, which when the Thames was at high tide filled to a depth of two feet with water. As the water came in, so did rats attempting to escape it, with extremely unpleasant consequences for anybody they found there. Fawkes, according to Ainsworth, refused to confess even after this experience.

Ainsworth's version of the Gunpowder Plot was very different from that which had dominated Protestant prop-aganda and historiography for nearly two centuries after 1605, and was the product of an intellectual milieu in which traditional anti-Catholicism was becoming a thing of the past for the novel-reading public. In his preface to the book Ainsworth summarised his main Catholic characters thus:

> In Viviana Radcliffe I have sought to portray the loyal and devout Catholic, such as I conceive the character to have existed at the period. In Catesby, the unscrupulous and ambitious plotter, masking his designs under the cloak of religion. In Garnet, the subtle, and yet sincere Jesuit. And in Fawkes the gloomy and superstitious enthusiast. One doctrine I have endeavoured to enforce throughout, – TOLERATION.

Ainsworth committed the book to 'that wider and more

discriminating class of readers from whom I have experienced so much favour and support', a sentiment which seems to have been fully justified. Ainsworth's novel surely symbolises a turning-point: for many educated people, the old function of the history of the Gunpowder Plot in supporting a Protestant, providentialist, and anti-Catholic version of England's past was redundant. There was now room for new interpretations.

Ainsworth's novel made Guy Fawkes an acceptable fictional character, and he began to appear regularly in the children's books, penny dreadfuls and serial publications. An example of these is a work which appeared around 1905, *The Boyhood Days of Guy Fawkes; or, the Conspirators of Old London*. This ended conventionally enough by referring to Fawkes as a 'misguided religious fanatic ... whose name still lives, and for ever will live, in abhorrence in the minds of Englishmen'. The whole tenor of the book, conversely, was to refashion the Gunpowder Plot as a straightforward adventure story for boys in which Guy Fawkes is presented essentially as an action hero, aided by a Sancho Panza figure in the form of a hunchback known, with no concessions to anything like modern political correctness, as Humpy. Guy was referred to by one of the characters in the novel as 'a rash, hot-headed youth, and unless he watches it well, he will come to no good', although 'it was a certain fact, and freely acknowledged in York, that Guy was one of the bravest youths to be met with, and people told him that if he followed in his father's footsteps he would, one day, be a great man'. In so far as serious history is touched upon in the chases, swordfights and shoot-outs which characterise the plot of this book, it reflects what was a growing consensus. The oppression of Catholics is noted, many sympathetic Protestant characters express a wish for toleration, and Fawkes is allowed an impassioned prayer for the restoration of Catholicism. James I receives what was becoming the obligatory bad press: 'his favourites ruled the country; and a disgraceful rule it was. But it is not our intention in this history to try the patience of our readers by an account of the manner in which the affairs of the state were conducted, or rather *mis*-conducted.' Amidst all this Fawkes is portrayed as a brave and principled figure, albeit a religious fanatic. And, interestingly in the light of some of the evidence from earlier plays, the anonymous author commented on how 'the majority of English people are under the misapprehension that Guy Fawkes was a Spaniard', and set out to put matters right.

Another staple of the Victorian reading public was the serious historical work aimed at the general reader, which might, as T.B. Macaulay's best-selling *History of England* demonstrated, achieve massive sales. Here too we can see how the image of the Plot available to the reading public might alter.

There were, of course, a number of books written specifically about the Plot, but the first of these to meet modern criteria on what 'proper history' might look like was David Jardine's *A Narrative of the Gunpowder Plot*, published in 1857. Jardine was a barrister and a Protestant, and had earlier published an account of the Plot and reproductions of the relevant trial records in a series called 'The Library of Entertaining Knowledge'. His work of 1857 was a scholarly study based on a wide reading of both printed and manuscript sources. Jardine took what was to become the standard line on the Plot. He commented that 'a contrivance so inhuman as the Gunpowder Plot can only be ascribed to the

baleful influence of fanaticism', but he also accepted that
Catholics in general had real grievances. 'The depressed condition of the Roman Catholics,' he wrote, 'resentment of the
wrongs they had suffered, the dread of further persecution
and, above all, perhaps, indignation at the faithless conduct
of the king, were motives sufficient to lead men to resistance and insurrection.' He also commented, as others had
indeed done before him, that the plotters were 'men of mild
and amiable manners, refined by a liberal education, averse
to tumults and bloodshed, and dwelling quietly amidst the
humanities of domestic life'.

General histories of England, however, offer insights
into how Gunpowder Treason was being represented to the
reading public at large. Widely read in its day, if now more
or less forgotten, John Lingard's *History of England, from the
First Invasion by the Romans to the Accession of William and
Mary in 1688*, first published in eight volumes between 1819
and 1830, summarised the position of the conspirators in the
following terms:

> With respect to themselves, they had certainly enter-
> tained the design laid to their charge: but whatever men
> might think of the fact, they would maintain that their
> intention was innocent before God. Some of them had
> already lost most of their property – all had suffered
> severely on account of their religion. The king had broken
> his promise of toleration, and the malice of their enemies
> daily aggravated their burdens. No means of liberation
> was left but that which they had adopted. Their only
> object was to relieve themselves and their brethren from
> the cruelty of the persecutors, and to restore a worship
> which they believed to be the true worship of Christ; and

for this they risked, and for this they were ready to sacri-
fice, their fortunes and lives.

Here Lingard, who was, a few pages later, to construct a
graphic description of a post-Plot anti-Catholic reaction,
was establishing what was to become the standard position
among popular historians over the late nineteenth and twentieth centuries, and one which was similar to that found in
some of the plays of the period: the Plot was reprehensible,
but it was understandable given the way in which Catholics
had been treated in Elizabeth's reign and the opening stages
of James's. In an age where religious toleration was regarded
as desirable, and secularism was on the advance, such an
interpretation seemed entirely appropriate.

It was the interpretation followed, to take a very perti-
nent example, by another historical best-seller, J.R. Green's
Short History of the English People, a massively popular work
which sold 32,000 copies in the twelve months after its publication in November 1874. Green provided a straightforward account of the Plot, and avoided moralising on behalf
of either party, other than remarking that 'the despair of the
Catholics gave fresh life to a conspiracy that had long been
ripening'. This position was also essentially that taken by
a rather more substantial historian, S.R. Gardiner, the man
who more or less invented English seventeenth-century
political history as we know it. In his magisterial ten-volume
*History of England from the Accession of James I to the Outbreak
of the Civil War 1603–1642*, Gardiner commented as follows
on the Plot:

The renewal of the persecution of the Catholics may
appear to the historian to be the inevitable result of the

claim of the Pope to universal authority, under the conditions of the times. It was not likely to appear in that light to the Catholics themselves. They would see no more than the intolerable wrongs under which they suffered; and it would be strange if there were not some amongst them who would be driven to meet wrong with violence, and to count even the perpetuation of a great crime as a meritorious deed.

This mood of even-handedness was to survive into the twentieth century. Winston Churchill, in his *History of the English Speaking Peoples*, first published in 1956, attributed the Plot to the 'disappointment and despair' which led a small group of Catholic gentlemen to contemplate desperate measures, and concluded that the main outcome of 'so novel and so wholesale' a treason was that English Catholics were subjected to 'immediate and severe persecution and widespread detestation'.

Mention of S.R. Gardiner raises another aspect of the historical treatment of the plot. In 1897 he wrote a rejoinder to a work published by John Gerard, a Jesuit, entitled *What Was the Gunpowder Plot? The Traditional Story Tested by Original Evidence.* Some years previously Gerard had published *The Condition of Catholics under James I,* a work in which his seventeenth-century namesake's narrative of the plot was reprinted, and in *What Was the Gunpowder Plot?* John Gerard attempted to completely overturn the conventional story. He argued that the Plot was essentially the work of Salisbury, and that, 'for purposes of state, the government of the day either for means to instigate the conspirators to undertake their enterprise, or at least being, from an early stage of the undertaking, fully aware of what was going on, sedulously nursed the insane scheme till the time came to make capital out of it'. Gerard was, in fact, building on what was a long-established Catholic counter-history of the Plot. The idea was certainly current, and not only in Catholic circles, in the seventeenth century, and Gerard cites a number of contemporaries and near contemporaries who voiced their suspicions or asserted their convictions over the point. It was also to surface in the eighteenth century, in an anonymous tract of 1765, for example. And, despite Gardiner's demolition of Gerard's arguments, the notion that the Gunpowder Plot was a creation of Salisbury and his creatures was to resurface in *Guy Fawkes: the Real Story of the Gunpowder Plot?*, published by another Jesuit, Francis Edwards, in 1969. Despite such efforts, it was the traditional story of the Plot which was to remain dominant. But it is obvious that, among mainstream historians at least, that story has been increasingly presented with minimum recourse to anti-Catholic comment.

TOWARDS 1859

Even among the preachers delivering their 5 November sermons, the mood was changing as the nineteenth century progressed. This process was, admittedly, slow and partial. On 5 November 1805 Ralph Churton, rector of Middleton Cheyney in Northamptonshire, preached a bicentennial sermon on the Plot before the University of Oxford gathered in St Mary's, the university church. Interestingly, Churton was directing his opprobrium at yet another statement of the Salisbury involvement theory which had appeared in a recently published history of Winchester, and both in his sermon and a printed appendix cited historical evidence against this interpretation. More conventionally, in his sermon he also gave thanks for a benign divine providence and reminded his listeners of the seriousness of the Plot: 'for barbarity of design and magnitude of the intended mischief, this monstrous conspiracy is without example ... then indeed, if the Lord himself had not been on our side, ungodly men had swallowed us up quick, when their wrath was kindled against us'. Churton also made some pointed comments about the spectre of Catholic emancipation. This pass had, however, already been sold when Edward Bickersteth, rector of Watton in Hertfordshire, delivered a sermon on 5 November 1842 to the Protestant Association gathered in St Dunstan's, Fleet Street. Bickersteth opened his sermon by deploring the way in which 'the wordly mind' might regard a celebratory Protestant commemoration of the Plot as 'a vain and feeble attempt to revive slumbering intolerance, and to cherish groundless alarms about dangers which are long past and gone'. To Bickersteth, 'we commemorate this day the happy deliverance of our church and nation from the gunpowder treason, and from Popish tyranny, and arbitrary power', and he went on to treat his hearers to an unrelenting rehearsal of the Catholic threat, in the process taking a swipe at 'the Infidel Poet Shelley' and linking the Greek Revolt of 1822 to prophecies in the Book of Revelation.

Yet even among anti-Catholic preachers a softer tone was developing. A year after Bickersteth preached in Fleet Street, Robert J. M'Ghee preached a Fifth of November sermon in Harold's Cross Church in the Diocese of Dublin. The day, M'Ghee reminded his listeners, 'was a day of thanksgiving for the most singular and providential deliverance of the king, lords, and commons of England, from the most singularly atrocious and wholesale slaughter that ever was meditated in the corrupt heart of man'. The Plot was not the result of any unusually criminal proclivities among the plotters, so M'Ghee argued, but was rather 'the result of the horrible nature of that antichristian system in which these men were educated'. Yet it was this observation which gave M'Ghee a distinctive line of approach. He was, as assuredly as any of those who had preached a sermon on any Fifth of November before him, convinced of the utter depravity and ungodliness of the Catholic Church, but he regarded individual Catholics, and especially those individual Catholics who were his poor fellow-countrymen, as victims of deception rather than as agents of Antichrist.

On that same day, 5 November 1843, Joseph Oldknow was preaching to the congregation of Holy Trinity Chapel, Bordesley, Birmingham. Oldknow admitted that 'it is, in many respects, painful to preach' about the Roman Catholic Church, noting in particular its 'corrupt additions to Divine Revelation' and the 'arrogant assumption of infallibility'. But Oldknow exhorted his listeners to remember the good things about the Catholic Church which had been preserved 'amidst all her corruptions', suggesting that 'my brethren we have sinned, grievously sinned, in the harsh and violent language we have been accustomed to hold concerning this church'. He pointed out that it was not by accident that he was voicing these sentiments on 5 November. This was a day of thanksgiving for the great deliverance of the discovery of the Gunpowder Plot, 'but I fear, however, that of late years the effect of its observing has rather been to influence our minds with rancour towards a portion of our fellow Christians, than to excite in them feelings of thankfulness to our Almighty preserver'. He urged his audience to 'mitigate the asperity and bitterness in which we have been prone to indulge', and ended the sermon in a plea for the maintenance of a spirit of unity and a bond of peace and love among Christians.

Oldknow's sermon apparently did not leave all of his hearers unruffled, and in the 'Advertisement' which accompanied its published version he was at pains to emphasise that he was not advocating anything approaching a rapprochement with the Catholic Church. Yet his sermon indicates how educated opinion was shifting. On the strength of the plays they went to, the novels they read, the books they derived their opinions about history from, and, perhaps, increasingly the sermons they heard on 5 November, enlightened Victorians were eschewing rabid anti-Catholicism and adopting a more liberal attitude. This held that the Gunpowder Plot should be remembered in as unpartisan a way as possible, and that the correct attitude to adopt to its history was to regret the atmosphere of religious intolerance that had both prompted the Plot and encouraged the plotters.

Eventually, in 1859, the service of commemoration was removed from the Anglican prayerbook, and the annual opportunity to draw upon increasingly distant history to encourage anti-Catholic sentiment was no more. The 5 November service was one of four special services which had been added to the prayerbook by the authority of the Crown, the others being Queen Victoria's Accession Day, the anniversary of the execution of Charles I, and the anniversary of the Restoration of Charles II. Many churchmen disliked these services, and from about 1840 it seems that they were far from universally observed. The mood was epitomised by a young clergyman, upbraided by his bishop for refusing to read the 5 November service, who excused himself on the grounds that 'it is not a church service but a state service, and I could not conscientiously read it'. Added to this opposition within the Church was that growing feeling that the anti-Catholic sentiments of the service to commemorate Gunpowder Treason were redundant, a sentiment shared strongly by Queen Victoria herself, who disliked such authorised attacks on her Roman Catholic subjects. Victoria's Accession Day was retained as a day of celebration, but the other three services were dropped from the prayerbook, apparently without serious controversy.

But there was a counterpoint to this drift towards the development of enlightened, liberal attitudes. As the popular historian G.M. Trevelyan put it, the Fifth was commemorated not only by being 'decorously celebrated in the church service', but also by 'democratic rites at the street corner in which the least mystical could participate'. Some of the participants in the street corner rites were demonstrating attitudes which polite Victorian society would have found reprehensible: the annual commemoration of Gunpowder Treason, that remembrance of divine providence and Catholic perfidy, was being replaced by the popular rituals of Bonfire Night.

5

THE TRIUMPH AND TAMING OF
BONFIRE NIGHT

On 4 November 1804 the London *Times* reported

> The great annoyance occasioned to the public by a set
> of idle fellows, going about previous to and on the 5th
> of November, with some horrid figure dressed up as a
> Guy Faux, and which assembling a mob, is the cause of
> many depredations and disorders; has very properly
> determined the magistrates to punish all such offenders
> in future. Yesterday therefore, five men and a boy were
> apprehended in St Martin's Street, with a cart, in which
> was a figure as the effigy of Guy Faux, and one of the
> party as a priest, habited in a white frock smock and a
> large wig, and the boy riding on horseback as the sheriff
> conducting the offender to the place of execution.

At some point in the late eighteenth century, in a process
whose timing and causes remain uncertain, Guy Fawkes
had emerged as the central figure in popular conceptions
of how the Fifth should be celebrated. By about 1800 it was
Guy Fawkes, not the Pope, who was most likely to be burnt
in effigy. At least one early nineteenth-century description
of popular customs, William Hone's *Every-day and Table*

19. An illustration by George Cruikshank for William Hone's Every-day
and Table Book, *1838, a guide to the customs of the period. This shows
what appears to have been the typical Guy of the early nineteenth century,
seated on what is more or less a poor man's sedan chair and, as yet, not
wearing the seventeenth-century costume that was to come. This image of a
popular, and juvenile, celebration of the Fifth is far removed from the civic
celebrations or Pope-burning ceremonies of the seventeenth century.*

Book, gives an elaborate description of what a Guy looked like, and also suggested that fashions in such matters as the clothes and headgear Guys wore and the accoutrements they carried were constantly changing. A play of 1793, *Guy Fawkes or the Fifth of November: a Prelude in one Act*, demonstrates that the type of Guy effigy familiar in Hone's book can be traced back at least to the late eighteenth century. In this play two 'chairmen' (i.e. carriers of sedan chairs) brought on stage a life-size figure of Guy Fawkes which they had sold, it was claimed, to one of the main characters in the drama for five guineas. The figure was subsequently burnt amidst fireworks and celebrations.

There is comparatively little evidence of how 5 November was commemorated over much of the eighteenth century, although such evidence as there is strongly reinforces the impression that, early in that century at least, Guy Fawkes was not the figure most likely to be burnt on 5 November bonfires. Early nineteenth-century accounts of the parading and burning of Guys can be compared to an entry in the *Weekly Journal, or British Gazeteer* of 10 November 1716, the year after an unsuccessful, and pro-Catholic, Jacobite rising:

> About 7 a-clock on the 5th of November last, a Detachment was sent from the Roebuck [an inn frequented by pro-government loyalists] to ... where the images lay; as soon as every man had his proper charge given him, and links lighted, Old Infallibility [the Pope] was brought out. Next came his unfortunate son, Perkin [the Pretender], drest in a black coat, scarlet stockings, and a pair of wooden shoes on his left shoulder; their old friend the devil serv'd for their life guard, and brought up the rear. In this manner

we march'd along ... our company increas'd to some
thousands; we continu'd ... back to our bonfire, which
we went round, and then committed [the effigies] to a
fiery tryal, amidst the acclamations of a vast concourse
of people, crying no popery, no pretender, king GEORGE
and the royal family for ever.

There is no mention of an effigy of Guy Fawkes here, and
neither is there in another piece of evidence from about
the same date. In 1718 a short farce was published satiris-
ing Thomas Bradbury, a controversial nonconformist minister who was a prolific author of 5 November sermons. The
playlet, which turned on Bradbury's having been burnt in
effigy at Wakefield, is very politicised, its basic line (appropriately given the individual who was the target of its satire)
being that honest, patriotic, Protestant 5 November celebrations were being taken over by nonconformist fanatics. In
one scene appear those images that were destined to be
burnt on the Fifth: 'effigies of the Pope, devil, Pretender, and
several in the habits of the popish order'. And, again, no
Guy Fawkes.

Such shards of evidence aside, there are few clues as to
how the Fifth was celebrated over much of the eighteenth
century. But we do have considerable evidence on how 5
November celebrations developed and took on a whole
new political resonance 3,000 miles to the west, in Britain's
American colonies.

POPE DAY

The early Puritan settlers in New England, conscious that
they had enough providences of their own to celebrate, and

suspicious of the popular elements in Gunpowder Treason celebrations, paid little attention to 5 November. Moreover, the relatively relaxed Anglicanism and the existence of a large, and generally tolerated, Catholic presence in Maryland and Virginia did not make those two colonies fertile ground for celebrations of the Fifth. Mention of the apprehension of boys lighting bonfires on 5 November 1662 in Boston (their parents were fined) suggests that an underground tradition of commemorating the Fifth existed, but such references are rare. Yet by the early eighteenth century full-blown celebrations on the Fifth, known, appropriately given the nature of the rituals in England at that time, as 'Pope Day', occurred regularly (and William Hone's *Every-day Book* suggested that in England, too, boys celebrating 5 November might call it 'Pope Day'). Thus in New York City on 5 November 1737 the local elite gathered, including the members of the Council, assembly and corporation, along with 'the principal gentlemen and merchants', to join the Lieutenant Governor in drinking loyal healths to King George II, the windows of New York being illuminated as they would have been in London. There is no certainty as to when Pope Day established itself in the colonies, but an intelligent guess would be that it did so at the time of the Exclusion Crisis and the political upheaval which preceded and accompanied the Glorious Revolution in England. Certainly the colonies all experienced considerable turmoil between the late 1670s and the early 1690s, with fear of a local Catholic plot being exacerbated by the more immediate threat of the French and their Native American allies.

As might be expected, Pope Day celebrations were not restricted to New York's elite drinking healths to the monarch. A few years later, it was common for 'a large body of the mobility' to parade through the city's streets with, as in England, effigies of the Pope, the devil, and the Jacobite Pretender. As a young lawyer, James Otis, who was to become prominent in Massachusetts Bay politics as an opponent of British policy in the 1760s, defended a group of youths from Plymouth, Massachusetts, who had forced homeowners to illuminate their windows on Pope Day and broken the windows of those who did not comply. This was probably typical of the sort of disorder which marked Pope Day, and it is interesting that Otis should describe what had happened as 'a common, annual frolic, undertaken without malice, and conducted without substantial injury'.

But in nearby Boston this 'annual frolic' had assumed a deeper significance. By the early eighteenth century, workmen and apprentices from the rival working-class North and South Ends would parade with carts carrying effigies of the Pope, the Pretender and the devil, with many of the boys participating dressed as devil's imps. Each cart had a stage on it, and, as a later account put it:

At the front of the stage was a large lantern of oiled paper, four or five feet wide and eight or nine feet high. On the front was painted in large letters, 'the devil take the pope'; and just below this 'North end forever' or 'South end forever'. Behind the lantern sat the pope in an arm chair, and behind the pope was the devil standing erect with extended arms, one hand holding a smaller lantern, the other grasping a pitchfork. The heads of pope and devil were on poles which went through their bodies and the stage beneath. Boxed up out of sight sat a boy whose mission was to sway the heads from side to side as fancy suggested.

Those in attendance often had blackened faces or wore masks, and would collect money from the houses of the better off. There was a great rivalry between the North End and South End parades, and the two would fight and try to seize the other's Pope to take and burn with their own. The two groups became more structured, each having a leader who organised the parade and directed any fighting. In 1752 a seaman died in a brawl in Boston on Pope Day, and in 1764 a boy was run over and killed by one of the carts.

This account of the transference of an English custom to the colonies, and its adaptation when it arrived there, would be interesting enough. What makes it doubly significant is that the Pope Day rituals gave plebeian Bostonians a schooling in demonstrating and crowd organization which was, from the mid 1760s, channelled into the growing political turmoil which prefaced the American Revolution. The crucial development was the attempt to impose the Stamp Act in 1765. This sought to impose duties on goods and services, among them legal documents, in Britain's American colonies in order to meet military expenses. Debates about the right of Parliament to tax the colonies escalated into wider discussions of political liberty and the colonists' status, and to mob violence. And that mob violence had its beginnings in Boston. The body of merchants and master craftsmen who called themselves the Loyal Nine (later the Sons of Liberty) persuaded the leaders of the North and South End Pope Day organizations to support their campaign against the Act with mass demonstrations, and in the summer of 1765 mob action forced the town's stamp distributor, a local merchant, to resign. The popular protests in Boston were widely reported in newspapers throughout the colonies, and similar disturbances occurred in many places, disturbances which frequently adopted the symbolism and rituals of Pope Day. These crowd actions were just the first in a series of popular demonstrations which were to accompany the various stages of the run in to revolution. However, like their equivalents in Britain, patrician politicians in the colonies, whilst recognising its usefulness in the short run, were nervous of giving the mob too much licence, and it is instructive to note that in 1775 George Washington forbade the officers and soldiers under his command from participating in 'that ridiculous and childish custom of burning the effigy of the pope'. By that date Pope Day was apparently in decline, although there is evidence of its continuation well into the nineteenth century. But as events in Boston had demonstrated, the Fifth had, in the colonies, proved itself adaptable to meeting the needs of yet another set of changing political circumstances.

BONFIRE NIGHT AND PUBLIC ORDER

Possibly the actions of the Boston mob give clues how the Fifth was celebrated on a popular level in eighteenth-century England. In some towns at least, local authorities were becoming alarmed at crowd disturbances on 5 November, while the mob reacted by seeing their celebrations as traditional customs to be defended. In November 1779 there was an attempt to ban bonfire celebrations in the town square of Horsham in Sussex. The following sentiments were pasted up on Horsham Town Hall:

> Man, if you will believe us in advising you for your own good, all you that have the least hand in trying to prevent the fire and fireworks in the town would best come off, for it is determined between us to have a fire of some

sort, so if you will not agree to let us have it in peace and quietness, with wood and faggots, we must certainly make some fire of some of your houses, for we don't think it a bit more sin to set your houses afire, and burn you in your beds, than it is to drink when one is thirsty. We don't do this to make a talk and chavash [chatter] about town only, but so sure it is wrote on paper, so sure by God Almighty we are in earnest. For we should desire no better diversion than to stand at a distance and see your houses all in flames. Gentlemen, we shall take no money nor anything else to go out of the square, for this is the place we have fixed upon.

For about the century following this expression of defiance to authority, the Fifth became a source of concern over public order in many parts of England.

The capital was not exempt. On 7 November 1853 a letter was published in *The Times* from a correspondent signing himself R.H. He lived in the vicinity of Tower Hill, where, he claimed, every year on 5 November a crowd of perhaps 15,000 persons assembled 'strictly for the purpose of robbery, brutal ruffianism, and to let off fireworks'. During the six years he had been resident there, claimed R.H., every Bonfire Night he had

been a witness in the metropolis of a sight unparalleled for ruffianism, theft, and riotous conduct in any other civilized city…During my travels, several years, in many principal cities in the four quarters of the globe, I have never met with such a consolidated mass of villainy; from all appearances every third person is a regular cadger or thief.

This particular year, he continued, his child was saved, 'almost by a miracle', from having his brains knocked out 'by a large oyster shell being hurled with great violence by some miscreant in the crowd', although his wife, who caught the full force of the missile, was badly stunned by it. The house of one of his neighbours was pelted with stones for two hours by 'a vagabond mob' of 8,000 people, and all its windows were broken, while the crowd set alight the house, and another neighbour had his house set on fire; 'And I protest', wrote R.H., 'that no attempt was made by the police to stop the scoundrels'. In London as elsewhere, popular celebrations on 5 November were becoming a public order issue.

Nowhere was this more true, and in few places is the issue better documented than in the town which is still renowned for its robust celebrations on the Fifth, Lewes in Sussex. Celebrations there had been noted from the time of the Exclusion Crisis in 1679, when we have a description of a 5 November procession which included 'Guy Faux and his dark lanthorne'. But by 1785 they were being interpreted in terms of popular disorder. In that year local respectable opinion was concerned with the safety aspects of the enormous amount of fuel which had been gathered for the bonfire. The authorities tried to intervene, the crowd resisted, the Riot Act was read, the magistrate who read it was knocked to the ground, and a riot began which continued until midnight. Nine ringleaders were later incarcerated in the local house of correction and fined 20 shillings apiece. In 1806 the celebrations were followed by eighteen arrests, in 1814 twenty-seven people were arrested, and in 1841 a police superintendent was bludgeoned to the ground when he tried to stop a blazing tar barrel being rolled through the town (a custom that had apparently begun in the 1830s). Official concerns were really focused in 1846, when a local magistrate, Sir Henry Blackburn, a man in his mid-sixties, was bludgeoned unconscious when he, too, tried to stop the rolling of blazing tar barrels. The next year, 1847, the local authorities swore in 170 special constables, arranged for two troops of lancers from Brighton to be stationed outside Lewes, and drafted in eighty members of the Metropolitan Police. There were no serious problems, although there were twelve arrests, with a further four coming later in November when the 'Bonfire Boys' took advantage of the removal of the forces that had been arrayed against them. The authorities seemed to be winning out through containment, and through a process of attempting to incorporate the popular defence of what was considered to be a legitimate popular custom into a form more acceptable to a mid-nineteenth-century urban elite.

In 1850, in Lewes as everywhere else in England, the Fifth was injected with a renewed significance. In that year a Catholic hierarchy was reimposed in England. On 6 November 1850 *The Times* commented on the situation in London:

> the recent unpopular assumption by the Pope of the power to confer papal dignitaries in this country has had the effect of giving quite a new character to the – of late years – almost forgotten celebration of the anniversary of 'Gunpowder Plot'. From an early hour yesterday morning the bystreets of the metropolis and its suburbs were rife with the effigies of Guido Fawkes...while crowds of urchins in all directions called upon her majesty's liege subjects in shrill tones to:-

20. *The reintroduction of a Roman Catholic hierarchy in 1850 drew this reaction from an issue of* Punch *in November 1850. Celebrations on 5 November of that year and the few years following were marked by rabid anti-Catholicism.*

Remember, remember, the 5th of November,
The Gunpowder Treason and Plot

There were demonstrations outside the Catholic cathedral in Southwark, while in Farringdon Market there were fourteen effigies, headed by a Guy Fawkes sixteen feet in height, which were processed through the Strand, Covent Garden, Bond Street, Whitehall and over Westminster Bridge to Southwark. Another large Guy was processed in the East End, and although the police suppressed the letting off of fireworks and lighting of bonfires in the city, 'very extensive bonfires and other demonstrations took place' in the suburbs. Among the effigies burned was that of Cardinal Wiseman, the learned, civilised and politically accomplished Irish Catholic clergyman who now, as Bishop of Westminster, headed the Catholic Church in England. These demonstrations were just one facet of a wave of anti-Catholicism which swept through England. This was even pandered to by the Prime Minister, the Whig Lord John Russell, the majority of whose government was under threat in 1850, and who was willing to play the anti-Catholic card to rally the votes of Whig Anglicans.

In 1850 Wiseman published his *Appeal to the Good Feeling of the English People*, a tract aimed at winning over moderate Protestant opinion. It did not win over the Lewes Bonfire Boys. Like their counterparts in many other towns, in 1851 they paraded effigies of Wiseman and the Pope before burning them, although here as elsewhere events on the Fifth were connected to a wider context of local religious and political power struggles. Nevertheless, the celebrations at Lewes were gradually becoming more controlled. Even in the 1840s it was noted that the Bonfire Boys were more organised, and from 1853 they began to be grouped into regular bonfire societies with sets of rules and their own recognised hierarchy. Each society paraded in a separate part of the town before joining in a grand procession. They each adopted specific forms of fancy dress, began to march with bands, and by the 1870s the 5 November celebrations in Lewes, although still boisterous, were on their way to becoming a town event rather than a confrontation between the Bonfire Boys and the local authorities. The fancy dress in particular became a matter of pride among the individual societies. Each included what became known locally as a 'Pioneer Front', a 'Second Pioneer Front', and 'Smugglers'. When the Lewes Borough Bonfire Society processes, Pioneer Front wear, as they have done for some time, Zulu warrior costumes, the Second Pioneer Front dress as Tudor ladies and gentlemen, and the Smugglers wear a blue and white striped jumper and a blue cap. The Commercial Square Bonfire Society has long marched in Lewes with its Pioneer Front dressed as North American Indians, its Second Pioneer Front as American Civil War figures, and its Smugglers in black and gold striped jumpers with red caps. Commercial Square attributes its Pioneer Front costumes to an interesting tradition. Apparently, some members of the society went to work on the railways in the United States in the late nineteenth century, were scandalised by the treatment afforded to the Native American peoples, and adopted their costume to publicise their plight. Such stories are difficult to prove. But the adoption of set fancy dress and the organisation of the Societies which set in from the mid nineteenth century was an important step in turning events on the Fifth in Lewes from what the *Sussex Weekly Advertiser* of 13 November 1849 described as 'riotous and brutalising orgies celebrated by a class of men taken from amongst the lowest ranks of society' into acceptable street carnival. By the 1860s on 5 November each year special trains ran from Brighton to Lewes bringing spectators to see the fun.

It took time for the anti-Catholicism to become muted. In 1870 the opening of a Catholic chapel next door to the pub used as a headquarters by one of the Lewes Bonfire Societies provoked a near-riot, and in 1901 the rather belated construction of a memorial to the town's seventeen Marian Martyrs helped sharpen traditional Protestant sensibilities. But, at the very least, other victims were joining the Pope, Cardinal Wiseman and Guy Fawkes to be burnt in effigy at Lewes on 5 November. As the international situation worsened during the approach to the Crimean war, the effigy of the Tsar of Russia was put to the flames on 5 November 1853, and other politicians and rulers were to follow him over the years. Local hate-figures joined them, the first of them a schoolmaster called Thomas Hopley, whose effigy was burnt on 5 November 1860 after he had escaped with a conviction for manslaughter for beating one of his pupils to death.

There were a number of other towns in southern England where diverging views on how the Fifth should be celebrated generated serious public order issues. One such was Guildford in Surrey, in the mid-nineteenth century a small market town where, during the 1850s and 1860s, a guerrilla war was conducted between the local authorities and the 'Guildford Guys', representatives of plebeian 5 November traditions. In 1851 Henry Peak, a young architect and surveyor, and a Chartist, arrived in the town, and was later to recall his first 5 November there. Going to post some letters in the town centre, he saw the 'surprising spectacle' of a large bonfire opposite Trinity Church, and noted that 'the whole

town was as if in a state of siege; every shop window not protected with shutters, and exposed glass on the ground floor
of houses, was barricaded; straw and manure heaped…to
prevent the penetration of fireworks'. Peak told how

> curiosity drew me closer towards the fire, where a great
> and lawless crowd was gathered; the chiefs, who were
> fantastically dressed in various costumes, were members
> of the 'Guy's Society', an organised body defying the
> police and officials of the town, and a saturnalia of mob
> rule was being carried on for the time being. Indeed, the
> whole place was at the mercy of the 'Guys', who gave
> orders to the mob by means of a horn, the blasts of which
> were understood and acted upon accordingly; and so the
> 'Guys' and their followers would sally forth from time to
> time for 'plunder' and return laden with spoil of fences,
> gates, doors and anything else which spite or fancy
> prompted them to make a raid upon and these were cast
> upon the fire with shouting and noisy demonstrations.

Peak, who was aware that large-scale celebrations of the
Fifth took place in London, was clearly totally unprepared
for these popular rituals.

Young Henry Peak was not the only person to leave
us with evidence of what happened in Guildford on 5
November in the early 1850s. In the immediate aftermath
of 5 November 1852 two clergymen complained to the local
magistrates about the events of that day. One of them, the
Reverend Henry Shrubb, recounted how:

> In the evening a number of people amounting to several
> hundreds came into the town from the neighbouring

villages, armed most of them with bludgeons, with their faces blackened and many I believe in women's attire ... In short the whole town was for these 3 or 4 hours in a state of complete riot, with no one to oppose their lawless proceedings, which were only terminated long after midnight by the men themselves being exhausted and worn out.

The mob had taken fifty yards of Shrubb's palings for their bonfire, threatened to murder the servant who was guarding the house, and meted out similar treatment to several of his neighbours; all this, Shrubb noted, taking place without any intervention from the police [the town had only three policemen at that time] or the local magistrates. The clergyman received little sympathy from the town authorities, and accordingly complained to the Home Office. In response to queries from central government, the mayor, a Mr Taylor, more or less confessed complete helplessness: prosecuting offenders in the past had done no good, as they simply escaped conviction, and there were so many participants in the celebrations that even calling in such locally available outside help as existed was pointless. The Home Office was not amused.

The next year, 1853, the town authorities anticipated 5 November by swearing in 300 special constables, most of them respectable local householders, and calling in assistance from the county constabulary and the Metropolitan Police. Accordingly, there were few problems. The following year, however, the Home Office, apparently unimpressed by the Guildford authorities and determined that they should sort their own problems out, refused to allow them to call on the Metropolitan Police, and 5 November there was a riot against the town's police and the special constables. There were widespread disturbances in the streets, the houses of tradesmen who had served as special constables in 1853 were surrounded and stoned, and the Riot Act was read. 'A stranger,' it was commented in a local newspaper, 'would have imagined himself in a country disturbed by anarchy and red republicans.'

The Fifth of November 1855 passed without serious trouble, but there were pitched battles between the police and the Guys in the two following years. Faced with what they clearly regarded as an impossible situation, the Guildford authorities more or less gave up, and on every 5 November between 1858 and 1862 the town was left to the mercy of the Guys. Thus the *Surrey Times* of 11 November 1859 complained that

> as the night advanced the scenes of disorder increased, and this sorrowful fact became too apparent: – namely that all authority had been abandoned, that government and rule had been suspended, and the whole town, with its property and its inhabitants was given over to an unjust, merciless, and ignorant mob, who greedily seize upon this occasion as the time to gratify their vulgar and plundering propensities.

The disorders that year included a full-scale attack on the town police station after the police inside had declined the mob's invitation to come out and fight. The year 1860 was another bad one, but in 1861, although, as the *Surrey Times* of 9 November put it, 'the police religiously absented themselves from the streets', the celebrations were better humoured, and, as in the previous year or two, it was noted that the Guys appeared to be better disciplined and showing more order within their disorder.

Even so, the situation was clearly unacceptable. Opinion on this point was sharpened in 1863 when a body of Guys disrupted civic celebration of a royal wedding by turning up to light a bonfire, and by a riot at the town's St Catherine's Fair on 10 October. On this occasion the deficiencies of the town's law enforcement agencies were demonstrated anew when a mob of 400 youths and young men roughed up respectable passers-by, an incident which prompted comments in the London *Times*. A new mayor, Mr Piper, vowed to end the 5 November disturbances, and met to discuss the situation with the Home Secretary. Accordingly, the town authorities prepared themselves for 5 November 1863 by calling in a military presence of 150 infantry and fifty dragoons, two companies of rifle volunteers (the Victorian equivalent of the territorial army), swearing in 150 special constables, and calling in the county police. There were no problems on the Fifth, but the Guys appeared and rioted on 21 November, two days after the troops had left, besieging the police station, beating up a policeman, and attacking the homes of those they knew to be hostile to their celebrations, destroying the front of the mayor's house in the process. But gradually the Guys were losing their hold. There were isolated problems in 1864, but the local police, carrying cutlasses and headed by a new and more pro-active superintendent, were able to contain them. Even so, the most vicious incident in the history of the Guy riots was to occur on Boxing Night 1865. A crowd of 150–200 people had been dispersed earlier that day, but a hard core of fifteen to twenty Guys, disguised and armed with bludgeons, turned out around 8 p.m. spoiling for a fight with the police. A lone constable was attacked, knocked to the ground and badly beaten, but others came to his rescue. The ringleader of the Guys, a cooper named Edwin Reeves, was arrested and subsequently sentenced to a year in prison with hard labour. There were no more riots after that in Guildford, and from 1867 a municipal fireworks display helped channel the old desire to celebrate Bonfire Night into a form more acceptable to local middle-class opinion.

Another town where 5 November was to prove a major battleground between the authorities and a plebeian tradition of celebration and excess was Exeter. Early in the nineteenth century Exeter had enjoyed traditional celebrations, with children letting off squibs in the streets in the weeks up to the Fifth, with the cathedral bells being rung on 4 November to commemorate William of Orange's landing in nearby Torbay, with guns being fired at 4 a.m. on the morning of the Fifth, and with large bonfires in the Cathedral Close. But over the mid-nineteenth century the commemoration of Gunpowder Treason in Exeter was to become more ornate, with pageants, processions, the burning of effigies, with, as in Lewes and Guildford, participants in these ceremonies wearing disguises or fancy dress. The catalyst here seems to have been Henry Phillpotts, Bishop of Exeter between 1831 and 1869. Phillpotts was a high-church Anglican and a high Tory, burnt in effigy within a few months of his enthronement on 5 November 1831 because of his opposition to Parliamentary reform (1832 was, of course, to witness the First Reform Act, and Phillpotts was not the only bishop to be burnt in effigy in 1831 for opposing reform). Exeter, and Devon in general, contained a large low-church presence which had good relations with local nonconformists. Accordingly, Phillpott's involvement in the Anglican revival, which was seen by many as creeping popery, and his

GOD SAVE THE QUEEN.

NO POPERY!   NO POPERY!!

ORDER OF THE GRAND PROCESSION,

For the Evening of Nov. 5th.

Rocket Brigade, to clear the way.

Forty begging bare headed Friars,

With Torches in their Hands to throw a Light on the Darkness of the Scene, and their own Iniquity.

The Inquisitor General on an Ass.

The Pope, Pius the Ninth,

In Full Pontifical Robes, carried in a Chair of State, on Men's Shoulders.

The Cardinal Archbishop of Westminster,

Dr. WISEMAN, in full Robes.

The BAND playing the "ROGUE'S MARCH."

The Twelve Roman Catholic Bishops of England.

Officers of the Inquisition, with Instruments of Torture for Heretics.				Officers of the Inquisition, with Instruments of Torture for Heretics.
Monks with Torches.	Bishop of Liverpool. / Bishop of Clifton. / Bishop of Birmingham. / Bishop of Plymouth. / Bishop of Southwark. / Bishop of Hagglestown.		Bishop of Beverly. / Bishop of Salford. / Bishop of Salop. / Bishop of Merioneth. / Bishop of Nottingham. / Bishop of Northampton.	Monks with Torches.

Romish Priests,

But in the Disguise of Puseyite Clergymen of the Church of England; as the Procession moves along, they will Chant the following old Song:—

"We stick firm to the loaves and fishes,
And hold fast with very great care;
It is clear if we give up our LIVINGS,
We cannot yet five upon air."
Sing fal de lal, &c.

"The world no doubt hypocrites call us,
And bid us act honest and fair,
But what can we do with our wives then,
For *they* cannot yet live upon air."
Sing fal de lal, &c.

Printer's Devils Tormenting.	Renegade Members from the Church of England, / With a Fool's Cap on their Head, a Bandage on their Eyes, / a Padlock on their Lips, and a Halter about their Necks.	Printer's Devils Tormenting.

The True and Faithful Citizens of Exeter will then follow and surround the Procession, giving expression to the Religious and Loyal Feelings of their Hearts, by shouting

"THE PROTESTANT CHURCH OF ENGLAND FOR EVER!
"DOWN WITH THE POPE AND POPERY!!
"THE QUEEN SUPREME!!!
"No PUSEYISM!!!!
"No TRAITORS WITHIN THE CHURCH!!!!!"

The Procession will enter the Cathedral Yard about Half-past Eight, and move round the Yard. The Procession will stop at intervals for those who like it, to kiss the Great Toe of the Pope, and then proceed to the Bonfire, where the Pope and Cardinal will be hanged on a Gibbet, and burnt with all the indignity heaped upon them which *their late daring* and impudent, but at the same time contemptible usurpation of power over the British people deserves.

The Bishops and the Inquisitor General, will then be kicked round the Bonfire, and then kicked into it, the Band playing GOD SAVE THE QUEEN, and the people singing—

"Frustrate their Popish tricks,
"Confound their politics,
"GOD SAVE THE QUEEN!"

21. Among the towns which experienced anti-Catholic mass demonstrations on 5 November 1850 was Exeter, with Cardinal Wiseman and the twelve newly installed Catholic bishops burnt in effigy. Here is a handbill advertising the event. Note that the targets of popular odium are not just Catholic bishops, but also 'Romish priests … in the Disguise of Puseyite clergymen of the Church of England', and 'Renegade members from the church of England'. The forces unleashed in 1850 were not merely anti-Catholic, but reflected divisions within the Church of England.

alleged attachment to Tractarianism, a high-church, Oxford-based movement which was opposed to liberalism and non-conformity, dismayed local religious opinion. The situation was exacerbated by the *Western Times* which ran a campaign against him. As elsewhere, matters were worsened with the re-establishment of a Catholic hierarchy in 1850. On 5 November 1850 the procession at Exeter included the effigies of the twelve newly instituted Catholic bishops, and in 1852 Phillpotts was burnt in effigy alongside Cardinal Wiseman. In the intervening year, 1851, the unfortunate bishop was burnt in effigy with reputed local Tractarians.

Tractarianism died out as a matter of contention during the 1850s, but, in Exeter as in Lewes and Guildford, the 5 November celebrations developed into a straightforward law and order issue. Exeter City Council had been created in 1836 as a consequence of the Municipal Corporation Act, and the Council was dedicated to maintaining order in the city. The old-style Bonfire Night celebrations, with unruly revellers in the Cathedral Close celebrating into the early hours of 6 November, the rolling of tar-barrels around the streets, and the letting off of squibs by children fitted badly with new-style notions of civic government. A notice by the mayor banning the letting off of fireworks on Guy Fawkes Day in 1843 was more or less ignored, and attempts to suppress the traditional celebrations that year resulted in a masked mob armed with bludgeons demonstrating outside Exeter police station and injuring several constables. There were further problems throughout the 1840s, and an attempt in 1852 to close down celebrations on the Fifth entirely led to disturbances in the course of which seventeen policemen were injured.

It was in 1867 that 5 November riots in Exeter reached

their zenith. This was a bad year, with hardship for many working people throughout England, and a political situation unsettled by the passing of the Second Reform Act. On 4 November inhabitants of the working-class suburb of St Thomas smashed shop windows and looted the premises of bakers in the Exeter city centre. On 5 November there were disturbances of varying degrees of intensity in neighbouring towns, and the Exeter magistrates decided to prohibit the customary bonfire in Cathedral Close. A mob formed and took control of the Close, driving out the special constables gathered there with a hail of stones and fireworks. The Exeter authorities, anticipating trouble, already had yeoman cavalry (again, the equivalent of a territorial army force) and regular infantry in place. The infantry cleared the Close with fixed bayonets, but the crowd simply returned when they were withdrawn, and the yeomanry proved useless, as their horses were terrified by the fireworks thrown at them. The mob then set off to rescue timber wagons which the authorities had impounded, and became involved in a bitter struggle with the county constabulary. These eventually gave way, but were replaced by the infantry, who cleared the mob at bayonet point, the disturbance eventually petering out in the early hours of 6 November. There was to be another Bonfire Night riot on 5 November 1879, when the authorities tried to prevent a wagon-load of timber being brought into the Cathedral Close from St Thomas. The wagon was guarded by men armed with cudgels, the police lost control of the situation, troops were again called in, and again the Cathedral Close was cleared at bayonet point in the early hours of 6 November. But as in Guildford, the plebeian desire for rioting and confrontation with the authorities on Bonfire Night seemed to be waning. There were no more

5 November riots in Exeter, and 1894 was the last year in which a bonfire was lit in the Cathedral Close.

There are probably numerous other stories which could be told of how celebrations on the Fifth were entwined with local political, religious and social issues. Sometimes these are easy to pick out: thus in Northamptonshire in the 1850s the Fifth became an occasion when Tories and Whigs, high-church Anglicans and Nonconformists attempted to appropriate an established date in the ritual year. Here too it was the reintroduction of the Roman Catholic hierarchy which seems to have caused serious problems, although here as elsewhere they arose within a specific religious and political framework. Northampton town was Liberal, with a strong nonconformist presence, while rural Northamptonshire was solidly Tory and Anglican, although with islands of urban Liberalism, among them Kettering, which contained a militant Strict Baptist group. The Liberals were less hostile to the Catholic hierarchy than the Tories, and so the latter, by playing on popular anti-Catholicism, tried to capture the Fifth and turn popular opinion against the Liberals. As in Exeter, there was the burning in effigy of Wiseman and others on 5 November 1850, and Tory-backed popular demonstrations were to continue on the Fifth in the early 1850s, with an effigy of Tsar Nicholas II being burnt at Towcester on 5 November 1854, the year the Crimean War broke out and further opportunities could be taken for displays of populist patriotism. But again as elsewhere, in Northamptonshire members of the local elite, including some men who had earlier backed unruly demonstrations on the Fifth, became alarmed at these displays of plebeian disorder and began to control and reform the festivities. Thus at Kettering in 1860 the Fifth was remembered with a display of pistol volley-firing and a fireworks display in the playground of Kettering Grammar School.

Sometimes we are confronted with reports of isolated incidents which may never be fully explained. On 5 November 1867 major disturbances broke out in the small North Yorkshire market town of Malton. From 6 p.m. crowds of men and boys assembled in the streets, and by 9 p.m. there were about 500 of them, who moved from street to street, 'setting all law and order at defiance'. The local police were powerless to stop them, and when they tried to do so 'they were hooted and mobbed, stones and fireworks being thrown at them'. The crowd broke up 'as night advanced, and the places where fireworks could be obtained were closed', although even after that 'guns and pistols were fired for some time, and one young man had his arm fearfully shattered'.

As well as these examples of mobs taking over the streets, the Fifth could be the occasion of acts of violence against individuals who attempted to stop the revellers preparing for or enjoying the festivities. In November 1862 Mr Isaac White, 'a respectable farmer aged between 50 and 60 years of age' from Manningham near Bradford, tried to stop a gang of about thirty boys and youths, 'most of them employed in worsted factories, dyehouses, and iron foundries' from removing his pales and fences to be used for building a bonfire. White told them to go, and took hold of a handcart they had brought with them. As soon as he did so, 'he was attacked by the whole gang of boys who, armed with poles, sticks and staves, knocked him down, kicked him, and left him bleeding on the ground and in a state of insensibility'. The doctor who was called to examine him expressed doubts about his recovery.

Such events are a reminder that, even outside the full-scale riots, the Fifth was a recurrent law and order problem for local authorities, the police and respectable opinion. Every year the police arrested people who let off fireworks in the streets, who begged too aggressively for pennies for fireworks, or sold fireworks without a licence (interestingly, the year after the Bonfire Night riot in Malton, the local magistrates forestalled trouble by refusing a licence to a local firework vendor). Thus popular commemoration of 5 November became a symbol of how social relationships and social control were changing in the nineteenth-century British town. In many areas (Guildford among them) local elites had organised civic celebrations on the Fifth across the eighteenth century. But increasing concerns about fire dangers, and deeper worries about public order and social discipline engendered by the French Revolution, meant that elites withdrew their patronage from such events, so that in places like Guildford and Lewes the celebrations, albeit with support and perhaps patronage from at least some highly placed individuals, passed into the hands of the lower classes. They regarded the Fifth, and their own way of celebrating it, as a traditional custom that should not be interfered with by new model town corporations and the new police forces these corporations created. It took a generation or so for urban elites to impose new ideas of order and respectability upon those they governed. In this they were helped by the fact that the lower orders were themselves changing. The *Surrey Advertiser* of 18 November 1864, commenting on the decline of the Guildford Guy riots, could claim that 'the working men of Guildford mindful of the self-respect that is expected of the working man in these progressive days turned a deaf ear to those who called for disturbances'. In

22. *The image of boys carrying a Guy in a chair was obviously becoming a familiar enough one to be enlisted in the cause of social and political satire. In the 1840s* Punch *was showing hostility to the contemporary 'Railway Mania', a period of heavy speculation in Britain's rapidly expanding rail network. The figure in the chair is almost certainly George Hudson, the York-based 'Railway King' who, by the mid 1840s, had over £300,000 invested in railway shares and owned companies which controlled over 1,000 miles of track. In 1847 the value of railway shares crashed, and hostility turned against large speculators like Hudson who had persuaded so many people to buy them.*

Guildford and several other places which had experienced problems on Bonfire Night (among them Chelmsford in Essex and Lewisham, then on the Kent/London border), local authorities provided entertainments on or around 5 November which satisfied a popular demand for spectacle in ways more appropriate to Victorian respectability than were the activities of the old-style Guildford Guys or Lewes Bonfire Boys. These, redolent as they were of the eighteenth-century 'Church and King' mobs, were increasingly redundant in a world of material progress, a respectable working class, trade unionism and professional police forces.

But, for contrast, let us turn to another town, Oxford, and a group of people who could not be portrayed as plebeian, university undergraduates. Here the story is one of upper-class hooliganism on the Fifth which can be compared to the plebeian hooliganism of Guildford, Lewes, Exeter and other towns. Initially, undergraduate celebrations of 5 November may have taken place largely within individual colleges. In an early incident, the aftermath of 5 November 1865 witnessed the whole of Merton College being gated following unruly celebrations around a bonfire in the college. In 1906 students at Brasenose let off numerous fireworks in the college, and lit a large bonfire, on which 'several seats, doors, etc.' were sacrificed. At Christ Church a large bonfire was lit in Peckwater Quad, around which about 200 undergraduates danced, while elsewhere in the college 'one undergraduate, disguised in a mask and wig, was found systematically breaking the ground-floor windows with a walking-stick'. An attempt by the college authorities to apprehend him was thwarted when other undergraduates gathered around him and he was able to slip away.

Oxford undergraduates also celebrated Bonfire Night in the city's streets and public places. On 5 November 1907 'a crowd of considerable proportions, in which town and gown were about equally represented', paraded up the High, and police intervention resulted in thirty arrests, eight undergraduates and four townsfolk subsequently being charged (the newspaper report of these events noted that 'as usual, the police took the hurly-burly in very good part'). Such customs persisted into the era of the Brideshead generation. In 1932 the *Oxford Mail* noted that 'The fights in the streets between town and gown were numerous' on the Fifth, and that 'the undergraduates would link arms and, walking along, would clear the streets. The ambition of the townspeople was to snatch off the mortar boards of undergraduates.' Helmets were knocked off policemen and boards were taken from buses, and the newspaper opined that 'these were only a few of the souvenirs which adorned the mantelpieces of the rooms in college the next morning'. These encounters were not always good-humoured: on the night of 5 November 1929 the Oxford fire brigade turned its hoses on a hostile crowd when its attempts to put fires out were contested. But, just as the Guildford working man changed in the late nineteenth century, so did the Oxford undergraduate in the late twentieth. The old-style undergraduate celebrations on 5 November, albeit ever more muted, survived into the 1950s, but then died out. On 7 November 1960 the *Oxford Mail* noted that Bonfire Night in the city had resulted in thirty-three people being charged with various offences; none of them were students.

FIREWORKS

So the old-style rowdiness of Bonfire Night, whether in the streets of Exeter or Guildford, or in Oxford college quadrangles, gradually died away. But it was not only replaced by organised civic displays. Most middle-aged or elderly Britons reading this book, as well as many from younger generations, will remember family celebrations, with a small bonfire in a back yard or garden, and with parents (invariably fathers) lighting the blue touch paper and retiring immediately, setting off the rockets, bangers, squibs, roman candles, catherine wheels and sparklers for the younger children.

For many people Bonfire Night was now a domestic event, a symbol of how domesticity was becoming a desirable and attainable entity in late nineteenth- and twentieth-century Britain. There were, of course, still public aspects. The sight has all but disappeared from British cities now, but up to a generation ago it was customary, in the weeks leading up to 5 November, for parties of small children to lurk strategically at street corners with effigies of Guy Fawkes, sitting in old prams or leaning against the wall, dressed to greater or lesser standards of ornateness, and beg a 'penny for the Guy' from passers-by. And, in an echo of the old communal celebrations, it was not uncommon in the 1950s to see street bonfires, especially on the bombsites which were commonplace in post-1945 Britain, and whose demise marks yet another change in the factors which have affected how the Fifth has been celebrated.

But all this reminds us that there is a vital element in the history of the Fifth which, so far, we have little discussed: fireworks. The seventeenth-century civic celebrations on 5 November, the squibs which Pepys recorded London boys setting off, the fireworks which Victorian mobs threw at the police and those other fireworks which urban elites provided in nineteenth-century civic displays, the fireworks ignited by fathers in family gatherings in the twentieth century: all of these remind us that fireworks, practically since 1605, have been inseparable from the celebration of the Fifth. So the history of Bonfire Night leads to another relatively unexplored theme, the history of the British firework industry. And here, too, the story is a more complex one than might be expected, and goes in some unexpected directions.

Initially many fireworks were home-made by amateurs, and this was to continue into the nineteenth century. Henry

Peak, whose encounter with the 'Guildford Guys' we have noted, was impressed to find them equipped with 'formidable and dangerous things – being immense squibs, many of them at least 12 or 15 inches in length and 1½ and 2 inches in diameter, and being chiefly loaded with gunpowder, and heavily rammed their force of explosion when discharged was tremendous'. The Lewes Bonfire Boys used an equally terrifying giant squib known as the 'Lewes Rouser'. Information on how to make fireworks had long been available. The first English book on fireworks, which drew heavily on earlier continental publications, John Babington's *Pyrotechnia, or a Discourse of Artificiall Fire-works,* was first published in 1635. It was followed by other works, notably *A New Treatise on Artificial Fireworks*, written by Robert Jones, a lieutenant in the Royal Artillery, first published in 1765 (there were subsequent editions with an altered title). By the nineteenth century, however, there was a wide variety of books aimed at young readers which would contain instructions for making fireworks along with other recreational activities. One such was *The Complete Conjuror; with the whole Art of making Fireworks. By the Wizard of the North*, published by that great printer of popular and ephemeral works, J. Catnach, around 1833.

But a growing demand for fireworks, especially on 5 November, meant that more fireworks had to be produced, and the history of firework production ran parallel to many other sectors of British light industry in the nineteenth and twentieth centuries. As with other types of manufacturing, fireworks were produced, especially during the run-up to Bonfire Night, as a sideline by people whose main employment lay elsewhere. Thus on 7 November 1854 *The Times* reported the injury of a London dairyman named Watson, who 'had been in the habit of making fireworks to be sold on Guy Fawkes Day'. The report continued that 'this season, it is stated, he has been more than usually busy', and had been obliged to work through the night with members of his family. An explosion occurred while Watson was out of the house, his wife and four children were killed, and he was badly burnt trying to rescue them. An essentially similar story was reported from the Huddersfield area two years later. A clothdresser named John Shaw had for some time 'been in the practice of making large quantities of fireworks for sale' on the Fifth, and was thus employed in his 'humble dwelling' along with his wife, son, daughter and seven-year-old grand-niece. They had two candles to provide light as they worked, and despite their precautions, a candle accidentally ignited some loose gunpowder which in turn set off a 70lb pile of powder in the room, along with 'other dangerous articles used in the manufacture of fireworks'. All of those working there apart from Shaw's wife were badly burnt, and Jane Ellen Barraclough, the seven-year-old grand-niece, was later to die of her injuries.

Early firework manufactories, frequently located in close proximity to private dwellings, suffered a similarly bad safety record. On 5 October 1852 *The Times* described an accident at a workshop in Finsbury, where 'it appears that a number of men and boys have been engaged in several days preparing a quantity of fireworks to complete a large order for Guy Fawkes day next'. A squib accidentally ignited, setting off a pile of gunpowder and other substances, resulting in three people being burnt, one of whom had already died of his injuries at the time of the report. On 29 October 1842 the same newspaper reported the death of a fireworks-maker called Pinner and two of his assistants in his house when 'a large quantity of gunpowder [which] had been placed in an upper room for the purpose of making fireworks for the 5th of November' exploded. Sheer bad luck might be a factor in these accidents, as when on 6 October 1855 *The Times* reported how at Toxteth in Liverpool, a fireworks factory where 'a number of men and boys were busily engaged in preparing fireworks for the approaching day of rejoicing' was struck by lightning. But in most cases safety was the issue. In October 1868 an explosion at a fireworks factory in Barnsley resulted in eleven deaths and a number of severe injuries. The jury at the subsequent coroner's inquest noted that 'there appears to have been no proper regulation in the conducting of the work, and that the sheds were unfit for the business'.

What made matters worse was that these small-scale manufacturers often worked from premises in the midst of residential areas. To cite yet another accident reported in *The Times*, on this occasion on 9 August 1847, an explosion occurred at the residence and manufactory of 'Mr Darby, the well-known pyrotechnic artist'. The explosion, which caused considerable damage in the area, could have been much worse: the report noted that 5–6cwt of gunpowder stored in an outbuilding failed to ignite, and that Darby had just dispatched £2,000 worth of fireworks to Vauxhall Gardens, the site of numerous firework displays. This did not prevent Darby's neighbours from requesting a local magistrate to intervene and stop Darby from following his trade 'in a crowded and densely populated neighbourhood'. They claimed that there had already been five or six smaller explosions in his works.

As so often in the nineteenth century, safety in the fireworks industry was enhanced by a blend of tighter government regulation and the emergence of large-scale manufacturers with purpose-built premises. Charles Thomas Brock, a well known organiser of large-scale displays, opened a factory at Nunhead which, according to one of his descendants, 'embodied almost revolutionary ideas regarding both the safety of the workers and the limitation of the result of any accident that might occur'. He was approached by the superintendent of the military Royal Laboratory at Woolwich to prepare a report on how the fireworks industry might be better regulated. His report was fed into the Explosives Act of 1875, which, among other things, sought to regulate both the manufacture and the sale of fireworks. Obviously this legislation could not be uniformly enforced, but it did provide a framework within which a better regulated fireworks industry could flourish. Thus another major fireworks manufacturer, James Pain, who had a factory in Brixton, moved his activities to a new and purpose-built factory at Mitcham in 1877 to comply with the Act. The firms of Brock and Pain were to enjoy a long existence as firework manufacturers, as did Standard Fireworks, founded in 1901 by the Yorkshire draper James Greenhalgh, and there were a host of lesser manufacturers, such as Lion, Wessex, Astra and Excelsior. Their products rapidly assumed the characteristics of modern factory production: standardised products, a wide range of choice, attractive packaging and advertising. The variety of fireworks available from British manufacturers was massive. Thus in the 1930s Lion offered, for a penny, bangers called Thunderflash, Thunderbolt, Big Bang and Champion Banger, while for a halfpenny boys could purchase the Zulu Banger, Little Demon and Mighty Atom. This has, of course, all gone now. Since 1976 Pain's has ceased to sell shop goods, but continues to provide fireworks for large-scale displays. Standard Fireworks were taken over by a Chinese company, Black Cat Fireworks, in 1998, Black Cat having already absorbed Brock's. Firework production, like so much else, bears witness to Britain's decline as a manufacturing nation.

But Bonfire Night, constantly adapting as it has for the past 400 years, lives on.

6

WINTER FIRES

5 NOVEMBER 2004

The North Yorkshire village where I live has an annual bonfire on 5 November. In 2004, as in previous years, from early October garden rubbish, old doors, wooden furniture (a parish notice had requested that settees and armchairs should not be placed there), old boards of one sort or another, in fact anything flammable which people wanted to get rid of, was piled on the usual spot on the green. When you bumped into people conversation normally turned to the bonfire. Inquisitive newcomers to the village were reassured that the event was worth going to.

On the day itself, in what many might deplore as an obsolete sexual division of labour, a number of the married women of the village came together to make large quantities of vegetable soup, in this as in previous years reinforced with a shot of curry paste, ready to be sold alongside hot dogs and burgers that evening. Selling food is a major way of raising money for next year's fireworks, and, after catering for 160 people in 2003 and selling out with many potential customers left hungry, the organisers had raised their target to 200 in 2004. Everybody looked nervously at the weather: the Vale of York was demonstrating its unparalleled talent for doing dank, but despite the odd drops of drizzle in the air, at least it wasn't raining. The bonfire, by now of a respectable size, was lit at about 6.30 that evening, and when it was going well there was the firework display, about £400 worth going up in smoke. Most of the village was out, from the elderly to the babies and toddlers who were held up to see the fireworks by their parents. Adults unencumbered by the very young mingled and socialised, the mass of locals being leavened by a sprinkling of people from the surrounding villages. Older children ran around, enjoying the chance to be out playing in the dark, while teenagers hung out being teenagers. At about eight, after the fireworks, a fine display of rockets and cascades let off by the organisers, people began to drift home, some going on to private celebrations in their gardens. The bonfire burnt on, and was still smouldering furiously the next morning. For whatever reason, no effigy, whether of Guy Fawkes or anyone else, is burnt these days. The longest-established residents of the village have no idea when the 5 November celebrations began, although they figure in their earliest memories of the village. So, a simple, small-scale commemoration of the Fifth, is now a traditional one, and one of the fixed points in the village's calendar.

Elsewhere, the celebrations on the Fifth are larger in scale and more ornate. The most famous take place in Lewes in Sussex, where robust merrymaking on Bonfire Night has been well documented from the early nineteenth century, and doubtlessly goes back much further. These days the festivities in the town are co-ordinated by the Lewes Bonfire Council, which oversees the activities of Lewes's six Bonfire Societies. Each society, some of which date back to 1853, when the first Lewes Societies were founded, represents a separate area of the town, has its own coat of arms, motto, headquarters (normally in a pub), and harks back to the late nineteenth century by retaining specific costumes for its 'pioneers' and for its 'smugglers', with their striped Guernsey sweaters. The societies are major institutions in Lewes, and their members spend time throughout the year planning for the Fifth, fund-raising and socialising. When 5 November comes, all process separately and then, with the exception of the Cliffe, join into a grand parade which passes through the town centre. The Cliffe, despite pressure in the 1950s, refused to join the united grand procession unless it was allowed to display its 'No Popery' banner, and, this request being refused, decided, as the Cliffe Society website puts it, that it was 'strong enough to stand alone'. This notwithstanding, the event, which has become a major attraction in the area (in 2004 some 45,000 people, supervised by 380 police, came into the town on 5 November), is marked by firework displays and, in particular, the burning effigies not just of Guy Fawkes, but also of modern celebrities (political and otherwise) who have attracted the odium of the members of the Bonfire Societies over the previous year. In 2004 these included the town's traffic wardens, symbolised by the burning of a giant parking meter, and deputy prime minister John Prescott, unpopular due to his attitude towards granting planning permission for a new stadium for the local Brighton and Hove Albion football club. Others in the recent past have included Margaret Thatcher, Ronald Reagan, Geri Halliwell, George Bush and Osama bin Laden.

Other towns and villages in Sussex stage similar, if smaller-scale, events, among them Hastings, Rye, Battle, Barcombe and (just over the border in Kent) Edenbridge. Here too the local Bonfire Societies plan their processions, bonfires and fireworks displays throughout the year, and here too effigies

23. *An artist's impression of the 5 November celebrations at Lewes in 1892.*
By this date the celebrations in the town had been tamed, and the old tradi-
tions of plebeian disorder canalised into a street carnival, exemplified here by
the fancy dress. But note the 'bishop' preaching to the left of the illustration,
and the figure of Guy Fawkes with his lantern and the Pope waiting to be
consigned to the flames in the background.

other than that of Guy Fawkes are consigned to the flames: at Edenbridge the 'Celebrity Guy' in 2004 was Tony Blair, represented by a thirty-foot effigy with, as a comment on the Prime Minister's foreign policy, Stars and Stripes under-pants. Most of these Sussex societies do not hold their cele-brations on 5 November proper, to avoid clashing both with the main event at Lewes and with those of neighbouring societies. But their celebrations can still be ornate. Thus the order of procession at Battle in 2004, organised by the 'Battel Bonfire Boys', was headed by a Chief Marshall, a 'Guy Cart', banner carriers, and groupings of representatives from other Bonfire Societies in the area, along with three bands. The celebrations at Battle cost £12,000, mostly provided by local subscribers, while the Bonfire Boys were able to claim that in 2003 they had raised over £5,000 for charity on the Fifth, with donations going to some fifteen community groups and other organisations. Other Sussex Bonfire Societies are equally proud of the sums they have raised for local chari-ties during their celebrations. Overall, despite the drinking and rowdiness which sometimes accompanies them, these are essentially community-based affairs, one of the great annual local events.

This degree of community input into Bonfire Night fes-tivities is not feasible in the larger towns and cities, but many local councils are willing to fund firework displays and bonfires on or around 5 November. At Cardiff, a fireworks display was held on Saturday 6 November 2004, the annual 'Sparks in the Park' spectacular staged in the city's Cooper's Field, with a non-traditional note being provided by enter-tainment from presenters from local Red Dragon Radio, boyband Phixx, and girlband 411. There were a number of events in Manchester, with a firework spectacular organised by Trafford Council, Lancashire County Cricket Club and the *Manchester Evening News* at Old Trafford, and with other displays at Heaton Park in Prestwich, Wythenshaw Park and Buile Hill Park in Salford, these last two also incorporating funfairs. At Carlisle, in an event organised and funded by the City Council and sponsored by CFM Radio, the University of Central Lancashire, and the *Cumberland News*, a crowd of 35,000 people saw a spectacular hour-long display involving 20,000 fireworks and the burning of a giant galleon afloat on a sea of light. Throughout the United Kingdom, in 2004 as in every other year, 5 November and the days around it were marked by fireworks displays and bonfires organised by city or borough councils, local Rotarians or other charity organisations, by schools and bonfire societies, and, of course, by families in their back gardens.

But again, as has become commonplace in recent years, Bonfire Night 2004 witnessed recurrent law and order problems, accidental fires, arson and accidents. On 18 September 2003 Royal Assent was given to the Fireworks Act 2003, a piece of legislation aimed at curbing a perceived misuse of fireworks. The Act begins by noting that since the millennium 'there has been increased concern about the use of fireworks, particularly with regard to their anti-social use. This is reflected by the large increase in complaints from the public relating to noise, neighbourhood safety and general nuisance from fireworks.' The government, here as elsewhere anxious to seem tough on crime, created by this legislation a number of offences which could result in a fine of £5,000 and/or a prison sentence, while the police are empowered to impose on-the-spot £80 fines for minor infringements of the Act. Under the Act, selling dangerous fireworks is illegal (fireworks, whether manufactured in the United Kingdom or abroad, should conform to BS [i.e British Standard] 7114). Also illegal are the following: selling fireworks to people under the age of eighteen; supplying the more powerful types of fireworks to the general public; possessing fireworks in a public place if aged less than eighteen; the possession of a category 4 firework by anyone other than a fireworks professional; and setting off fireworks after 11 p.m., exceptions here being made for 5 November, when fireworks can be discharged until midnight, and New Year, Chinese New Year and Diwali, on all of which they can be discharged until 1 a.m. The Act also set an upper limit of 120 decibels on category 3 fireworks, while in addition the Department of Trade and Industry laid down strict regulations for the conduct of public displays.

Local newspapers were, in the days running up to 5 November 2004, full of stories about the hoped-for effects of the new legislation. Many places anticipated a 'Bonfire Night Crackdown', in which police and local trading standards officials acted to prevent the sale of illegal fireworks and to stop youths from discharging fireworks in the street, or throwing them at people, cars and buildings. Local fire brigades, some of them fearful of attacks on firefighters trying to put out fires, issued a warning to potential troublemakers, particularly those planning to ignite bonfires before 5 November. Many areas reported a diminution of problems in the run-up to the Fifth. In Suffolk, the Ipswich *Evening Star* of 6 November noted that the previous night had been quiet, with no major problems, a situation which the divisional officer for the Suffolk Fire Service attributed to a combination of the high number of organised events and the new legislation. Even so, problems persisted on a national level. Children and adolescents continued to let off fireworks in the streets and other public places, some of them falling foul of the police, others needing treatment in local hospitals. As well as accidental fires caused by fireworks, there were the usual isolated incidents of arson. There were other problems, as at Newall Avenue in Stafford, where, in an echo of nineteenth-century mob hooliganism, a couple living in a bungalow had fifty feet of fencing torn up and used to make a bonfire by local youths. Throughout the country police and trading standards officials seized caches of illegal fireworks, the Liverpool police, for example, seizing five tons of them stored in a container at a farm near the city. Both the *Manchester Evening News* and the Birmingham *Evening Mail* ran stories on how they had sent fifteen-year-old girls out to buy fireworks, and that they had been able to do so despite the ban on selling fireworks to persons aged less than eighteen. In Birmingham, two of the four shops which sold fireworks to the fifteen-year-olds carried Responsible Trader Scheme certificates which stated that they would not break the law by selling to under-age customers. This is one of those occasions when an historical perspective provokes a sense of irony. These modern concerns, understandable and genuine though they are, are being engendered by a Fifth that is massively less rowdy than it was in many areas a century and a half ago.

Despite the new legislation, Bonfire Night celebrations for 2004 were marked by yet another escalation in concerns over the safety issues involved with fireworks. Figures released by the Department of Trade and Industry reveal that 1,136 people in Great Britain were treated for firework-related injuries in a four-week period incorporating 5 November 2003, over 300 more than had been similarly afflicted in the same period in the previous year. There were no deaths, and few serious injuries, but the figures were disturbing enough, not least because over a quarter of the total accounted for eye injuries. Against a population of 60 million, these figures do not sound excessive, but given the spread of a 'compensation culture' in Britain they are serious enough for those considering running organised fireworks displays. Indeed, the fireworks industry claimed that the number of smaller displays had dropped by 30 per cent primarily as a consequence of the higher insurance premiums faced by their organisers. And the Fifth involves other insurance issues. Insurance companies advised homeowners to check that their home insurance included protection from the effects of being hit by stray fireworks or rockets, while, given that many families are out attending organised events on the Fifth, homeowners were also warned to take extra precautions against burglary.

Yet further worries about safety on 5 November were to appear in 2004. These centred on the possible damage from rockets to low-flying aircraft. On 1 November 2003 an Airbus A321, flying at 560 feet over Hounslow during its approach to Heathrow airport, was hit by a firework, while on 5 November 2003 itself another Airbus was struck at 250 feet by one of several fireworks exploding around it as it approached Manchester Airport. This led the Civil Aviation Authority, fearing that aircraft landing or taking off might be seriously damaged by fireworks or their pilots distracted by them, to impose strict controls over firework displays. Under these controls, anybody envisaging letting off rockets which would rise more than 250 feet, or organising a display that would last more than thirty minutes, should contact the Civil Aviation Authority in advance and give details of the event in question. By 21 October 2004 the Civil Aviation Authority had received some 800 applications relating to displays planned for November of that year.

The impact of increased insurance premiums on small 5 November displays prompted a number of articles in the national press. In *The Times* Mick Hume thundered about what he termed 'The Health and Safety Plot to Blow Bonfire Night off the Calendar'. Arifa Akbar in the *Independent* asked 'Has Bonfire Night Had Its Day?' And in the website *Spiked*, edited by Mick Hume, Josie Appleton contributed a piece entitled 'Bonfire of Our Sanity'. The message in these three articles is an essentially similar one: a combination of high insurance premiums and government regulations is killing off the old-style community bonfire celebrations. Appleton described some of the main elements of the Department of Trade and Industry guidelines: there has to be a 100 metre by 50 metre 'dropping zone' for spent fireworks, which in effect prevents people from gathering around a bonfire; alcohol is prohibited, as it might make crowd control more difficult; only trained people can let fireworks off; and spectators are banned from bringing their own fireworks, even sparklers. She continued:

> Community bonfires used to be one of the few occasions for local people to get together. In my small village in Nottinghamshire, the bonfire was the only time that I would see many of my neighbours. There was no barrier around the fire, my small brother spent all evening waving sparklers, and my non-pyrotechnically trained dad set off fireworks. Behaviour that was completely normal only a few years ago is now ancient history.

Concerned by the encroachment of governmental controls, Appleton reflects that 'antisocial' is an official code for 'spontaneous', while 'safety' is another code for policing, for 'reining people in'. Hume struck much the same note, claiming that 'an old-fashioned Bonfire Night is now anathema to authorities that seem shell-shocked by the very idea of crowds of people enjoying themselves with alcohol and a little gunpowder', and expressed (one suspects) tongue-in-cheek concern that David Blunkett's laws against inciting religious hatred might curtail the celebrations at Lewes, where the Cliffe Bonfire Society still parade with a 'No Popery' banner.

Britain's Catholics are likely to remain undisturbed on Bonfire Night. The same cannot be said of the nation's pets, and another facet of the annual rituals surrounding the Fifth in present-day Britain are warnings about pet welfare. On a national level, the Royal Society for the Prevention of Cruelty to Animals lays down guidelines for pet protection on the Fifth, directed primarily at cat- and dog-owners. In 2004 the advice was to keep dogs on a lead in the run up to the Fifth, to prevent their making off if panicked by fireworks, while for Bonfire Night itself a secure room was recommended, preferably in the middle of the house, where the pet's bed could be placed. Other animals, like rabbits and guinea pigs, should, it was urged, be brought inside from their hutches. In Cheshire, the Upton-based vet and animal behaviour expert Sarah Heath was quoted in the local media as advising that dogs should be given a relaxing early evening meal of over-cooked brown rice laced with Marmite, although, prudently, she urged care if the animal in question was known to have digestive problems. Rising to a challenge, the United Kingdom pet industry came up with some more sophisticated remedies. CDs are on offer carrying the sounds of fireworks, gunfire, thunder and so on, in the hopes that playing them to animals will acclimatise them to such noises. Conversely, a firm called Cutefurries has been marketing a CD of soothing music (with high notes edited out) aimed at calming the nerves of stressed or excited cats and dogs. Another firm, Groovypets, has developed a range of 'Natural Aromatherapy Remedies' for pets in the shape of oil blends and sprays, to be applied about an hour before fireworks begin and then topped up as appropriate.

The trauma that Bonfire Night can cause domestic pets is familiar enough. Recently, however, it has been identified as a threat to a wildlife species: hedgehogs. A little before 5 November 2004 Britain's Wildlife Trusts issued a warning drawing public attention to the issue. The crucial point is that hedgehogs tend to hibernate in late October or early November, and that bonfires built in anticipation of being ignited on 5 November look like ideal hibernation nests for them. The Sussex Wildlife Trust urged that bonfires should be raked gently before being lit to allow for the discovery of any hedgehogs hibernating in them, and that any hedgehogs thus found should be moved to a ready-made hedgehog box. The Trusts also suggested that, if possible, bonfire organis- ers should create an alternative hedgehog home for any of the animals they found. One can all too easily imagine the reactions of a nineteenth-century Lewes Bonfire Boy to such sentiments: but it is worth remembering that the problem of hedgehog safety on Bonfire Night has entered Britain's national psyche sufficiently for it to be used, in the autumn of 2003, as a story-line in that longest-running of radio soaps, *The Archers*.

Current concerns are worsened by the way in which

Bonfire Night celebrations are no longer restricted to the Fifth. There now seems to be what might almost be described as a firework and bonfire season which stretches for several days on either side of 5 November. The old precision about what is being commemorated has long since been eroded, while the specific focus on 5 November is evidently getting more fuzzy. So, 400 years after the event, what exactly are we celebrating when we commemorate this failed act of terrorism? What do these celebrations really mean in the early twenty-first century?

WINTER FIRES

As a first step towards answering these questions, let us look back to a novel first published in 1878, Thomas Hardy's *The Return of the Native*. In a striking passage near the beginning of the book, Hardy described the 5 November bonfires on the fictional Egdon Heath. A group of men and boys had built a bonfire of furze some thirty feet high on the heath, and as they completed their work,

> Red suns and tufts of fire one by one began to arise, flecking the whole country round. They were the bonfires of other parishes and hamlets that were engaged in the same sort of commemoration. Some were distant, and stood in a dense atmosphere, so that bundles of pale, strawlike beams radiated around them in the shape of a fan. Some were large and near, glowing scarlet red from the wounds in a black hide ... Perhaps as many as thirty bonfires could be counted within the whole bounds of the district; and as the hour may be told on a clock-face when the figures themselves are

invisible, so did the men recognize the locality of each fire by its angle and direction, though nothing of the scenery could be viewed.

As the fires blazed up, Hardy had his protagonists entering a mystical universe. 'It seemed,' he wrote, 'as if the bonfire-makers were standing in some radiant upper storey of the world, detached from and independent of the dark stretches below.' These Wessex bonfire-makers were thus transported back into a distant, mystical past:

> It was as if these men and boys suddenly dived into past ages, and fetched therefrom an hour and deed which had before been familiar with the spot. The ashes of the original British pyre which blazed from that summit lay fresh and undisturbed in the barrow beneath their tread. The flames from funeral piles long ago kindled there had shone down upon the lowlands as these were shining now. Festival fires to Thor and Woden had followed on the same ground and duly had their day. Indeed, it is pretty well known that such blazes as the heathmen were now enjoying were rather the lineal descendants from jumbled Druidical rites and Saxon ceremonies than the invention of popular feeling about the Gunpowder Plot.

The tone which Hardy set here was one which was to achieve a certain currency in the years around 1900, and which is still with us. There was a recurrent notion that the 5 November celebrations had been grafted on to earlier celebrations stretching back to pre-Christian times, with Hallowe'en, the old Celtic Samhain, as the most likely begetter of celebrations on the Fifth. These ideas have enjoyed a brisk rebuttal

24. *Lewes, 5 November 2001. The Cliffe Bonfire Society Procession, with the effigies of Pope Paul V (the Pope at the time of the Gunpowder Plot) and Guy Fawkes heading for the flames.*

from the historian David Cressy. The Fifth, he argued, may have replaced All Saints' Day as an early winter festival, but there was no connection for southern and midland England between the commemoration of 5 November and any pre-existing bonfire festival. But the notion remains embedded, and may have some important implications for the future of festivities on the Fifth.

To see the direction in which things may be going, let us consider another of those places where a strong and individualistic tradition of remembering the Fifth of November survives, Ottery St Mary in Devon. At the centre this township's Bonfire Night celebrations are rituals involving blazing tar-barrels. These may well once have been a common feature of celebrations on the Fifth – they were certainly present in the nineteenth century at Exeter, which is close to Ottery St

Mary, and at Lewes – but modern concerns for public safety mean that they now rarely figure in Bonfire Night celebrations. At Ottery St Mary things are different. Celebrations on the Fifth start there at 4 a.m., when people emerge to fire 'cannon', lengths of piping stuffed with gunpowder which obviously hark back to the old-style 'Lewes rousers' and the giant squibs which Henry Peak saw at Guildford in the 1840s. This process is repeated at 1 p.m. and 4 p.m. After that, the fun with the barrels begins. Barrels are soaked in tar for weeks before the Fifth, ready for ignition on the great day. In the late afternoon children and women participate, but after about 8 p.m. adult male 'barrel-rollers' take over. There are seventeen barrels, each sponsored by a local pub, and those taken up by the men weigh at least thirty kilograms. Despite the name of the ritual, the barrels are not rolled, but carried, spurting flame and sparks, on the shoulders of the men, who normally use only homemade hessian gloves for protection. Crowds gather on the street (buses bring spectators in from Exeter) and the 'barrel-rollers' set off with their loads through the streets, taking pride in their ability to carry the fiery barrels, with others jostling to take them off them. Latterly, celebrations begin on 31 October, Hallowe'en, with what is by now a traditional procession of floats through the town, complete with a Carnival Queen and Princesses. On the night of the Fifth itself, as well as the barrel-rolling, there is a bonfire with a Guy, and also a funfair and vans selling the usual foodstuffs.

The history of the celebrations at Ottery St Mary would probably reveal a story of plebeian festivity and respectable containment similar to those experiences at Lewes, Guildford, Exeter and other places over the nineteenth century: certainly there is a tradition that at some point around 1900 an incident occurred in which police sent from Exeter to prevent the celebrations were stopped by the local crowd, who threw the constabulary's horse-drawn vehicle into the river Otter. But, currently, roots for the ceremony akin to those traced by Hardy for the fictional Egdon Heath have been claimed for Ottery St Mary. What is in effect the official website for the barrel-rollers suggests that although opinion on the origins of this festival of fire is divided, 'the most widely accepted version is that it began as a pagan ritual that cleanses the streets of evil spirits'. Another site, describing itself as 'America's Gateway to the British Isles', informs those visiting it that 'this is an extremely ancient tradition, possibly older than that of the unhappy Guy Fawkes himself. Fire festivals around the time of Hallowe'en are deeply rooted in British folklore and have been connected with the ritual burning of witches.' David Cressy rejected the existence of fire festivals around early November for most of England, while, for my part, fifteen years of researching the history of witchcraft in England leaves me with no example of 'the ritual burning of witches' to bring to mind. But what matters is that these notions are evidently gaining currency. The historian Ronald Hutton records giving assistance on 5 November 1990 to a scorched 'barrel-girl' at Ottery St Mary, who told him that she participated in the barrel-rolling to chase away evil spirits from her town at the beginning of winter. At about the same time 'bonfire boys' at Battle in Sussex told Hutton that their celebrations were descended from the fire rituals which marked the Celtic New Year. This last comment raises the problematic issue of the Fifth's relationship with Hallowe'en: for if the commemoration of 5 November filled a gap left by the weakening of All Saints' Day in the seventeenth century, there is little doubt that Hallowe'en is currently replacing Bonfire Night as the major British winter-greeting festival. In November 2004 it was reported that spending on Hallowe'en in Britain that year had topped £100,000,000, more than the sum spent on Bonfire Night.

Extravagant claims have been made for Hallowe'en. There is a widespread consensus that it developed from the Celtic festival of Samhain. Samhain marked the beginning of winter, just as the other great Celtic festival, Beltane, corresponding roughly with May Day, marked the beginning of the summer. Samhain, so the standard pagan interpretation runs, was a time when 'the gates between this world and the next were open. It was a time of communion with the spirits of the dead, who, like the wild autumnal winds, were free to roam the earth'. It has been argued that the Christian feast of All Souls was based on this earlier, Celtic tradition, but that Hallowe'en, the night when the dead are meant to walk, and other supernatural beings appear on earth, is essentially a pre-Christian survival. The problem is, of course, that lack of any definite early evidence makes it difficult to assess exactly what was done or thought about at Samhain, while it is equally plausible that the Hallowe'en customs of the British Isles, for which we have occasional references from the sixteenth century onwards, might equally well be folkloric reworkings of the Christian feast of All Souls. But what remains clear is that in many places the old customs included the lighting of bonfires and the holding of celebrations around them. It is this which has led observers from the late nineteenth century onwards to the erroneous conclusion that Bonfire Night is based on the old Hallowe'en (and, by extension) Samhain bonfires.

But whatever the ancient origins of Hallowe'en, the modern Hallowe'en owes almost everything to modern practices in the United States. Hallowe'en is now one of the biggest cel-

25. Lewes, 5 November 2001. The Cliffe Bonfire Society always begins the evening of the Fifth with barrel runs, and here the Society's ladies' run commences in Cliffe High Street. In the early nineteenth century, in Lewes as in other towns, blazing tar-barrels were rolled through the streets, and later in Lewes were hauled at the end of each society's procession, making this modern practice an interesting example of the reinvention of an old tradition.

ebrations in the United States, and it is in the nature of things that Britain, and by extension the rest of the world, should follow suit: the modernised version of the festival is even being celebrated by the French, who really ought to know better. One is aware that there were traditional Hallowe'en rituals, often involving bonfires, and often with overtones of contacts with (or the need to avoid) supernatural beings or the spirits of the dead. These rituals were very different from the modern ones, where the nearest thing to a supernatural being in evidence is the great god consumerism. It is now very rare, although not wholly unknown, to see children out on the streets of British cities begging pennies for the Guy. But children and adolescents are frequently seen out trick-ortreating, a phenomenon which was absent from my London boyhood in the 1950s, and which, in some of the rougher parts of Britain, has assumed something of the character of begging with menaces. So here we have another symptom of the Americanisation of British culture: the festival with which we are being encouraged to mark the beginning of winter, in its widely accepted form, owes almost everything to an American model.

This is a pity, not least because the Fifth was a uniquely British, or perhaps more accurately English, event: nobody else had it. I have been aware, throughout the writing of this book, that I have concentrated on the English experience, and doubtlessly many readers could add their knowledge and memory of Guy Fawkes celebrations in other parts of the British Isles, as well as (to take the most obvious examples) Australia, New Zealand and Canada. One has a feeling that Bonfire Night celebrations used to, and perhaps still do, crop up in unexpected places. On 6 November 1957 the anthropologist Daniel J. Crowley, then at Fresh Creek, Andros Island, in the Bahamas, along with a number of out-of-season tourists, was informed by a small boy that 'we go burn a guy tonight'. At about 6 p.m. a dancing procession of men and boys, complete with local drums, danced through the grounds of Fresh Creek's hotel to a club frequented by locals, and, after waiting for a film being shown there to finish, danced around and then burnt on a bonfire a white-faced effigy in European clothes. When questioned, the participants explained that they normally held their celebrations on the Fifth, but had postponed them for a day in deference to the funeral of a local notable. They were a little uncertain about where the ceremony originated – 'It's a thing we having from England, mon.' One, however, informed

Crowley that 'it something we have from the loyalists', that is, supporters of British rule who had been on the losing side in the American War of Independence and had evidently brought Pope Day with them when they came as exiles to the Bahamas in 1783. One wonders how many similar tales could be told.

But now, perhaps, the Fifth in anything like its traditional form has had its day in Britain. There are still those who defend it. Martin Kettle, writing in the *Guardian* on 5 November 2003, identified Bonfire Night as the real 'Festival of Britain', in the sense that it was 'the one surviving national celebration which is truly popular, in the sense of belonging to the people', and that it had the added advantages of being impervious to being taken over by television and that largely escaped the commercialism accompanying 'the now much vaunted Halloween'. But studying the history of the Fifth makes one wonder how appropriate celebrating it is in a modern, secular society. The Fifth entered the national calendar as a commemoration of a Catholic plot to blow up the King of Great Britain and his heirs, to destroy the English Parliament, and replace a Protestantism to which most of the English were attached in 1605 with what was increasingly being seen as an alien and tyrannical Roman Catholicism. The continuation of 5 November as a day of festival owed much to its being included in the Anglican Prayer Book as a day of commemoration for two and a half centuries after Guy Fawkes and his fellow conspirators died. By the time this commemoration was discontinued, of course, Guy Fawkes had become an iconic figure, maybe even something of a hero. In continuation of the more tolerant attitude set in motion in the nineteenth century, I doubt if many of those attending bonfires or firework demonstrations on or around the Fifth these days have any great animus against Catholics. One wonders how many of them have any clear grasp of what the Gunpowder Plot was actually about. Apart from being something which British people do, it is difficult to see how Bonfire Night reinforces British national identity in the way in which it reinforced English national identity in the late seventeenth century.

THE FUTURE OF THE FIFTH

But these considerations bring us to pondering the significance of Bonfire Night for modern Britain and, by extension, for other western democracies, the United States included. Since the late nineteenth century, in mainland Britain at least, nobody in a position of authority has been encouraging the English to hate and fear Catholics. But people in positions of authority have, over the last sixty years or so (to look back no longer) advised us to turn our fear and loathing against other targets. For forty years after 1945 it was the Eastern Bloc, the Communist powers, who were aiming to destroy western democracies and whose agents were everywhere. With the collapse of Communism around 1990, amidst the general rejoicings and the self-congratulatory euphoria that capitalism and western democracy had triumphed, the more thoughtful inhabitants of the West, and one hopes all historians worth their salt, wondered whom we were going to find ourselves being encouraged to hate and fear next. Islam provided an obvious and not totally unqualified candidate. Famously, Francis Fukuyama proclaimed that the triumph of western capitalism and western liberal democracy signalled 'The End of History': one suspects that those who planned and

26. Perhaps especially for children, Hallowe'en is overtaking Bonfire Night in modern Britain. Here two Edinburgh boys have some Hallowe'en fun on 31 October 2004. Although they are clearly enjoying themselves, one feels that what they are up to has little to do with traditional Scottish Hallowe'en customs.

executed the attacks of 11 September 2001, or the bombing of the Madrid railway, or the bombing of the London transport services on 7 July 2005, had other ideas about the fate of history and where it might be going.

Historians should avoid facile comparisons between the past and the present. Conversely, the parallels between the position Britain (along with other western states) currently enjoys vis-à-vis Islam and that enjoyed between England vis-à-vis Catholicism between the mid-sixteenth and the mid-eighteenth centuries are intriguing. There is the fear of an alien ideology which most people, at best, only half understand. There is the fear that this ideology has at its command forces dedicated to the destruction of our political system.

27 (left). Claiming Guy Fawkes (I) . The pub sign for the Guy Fawkes Hotel (formerly Young's Hotel), High Petergate, York: Fawkes and his image live on! 28 (right). Claiming Guy Fawkes (II). 32–34 Stonegate, York. The original buildings are gone, but detailed research has suggested that this is the site of the house where Guy Fawkes was born and brought up, close to St Michael-le-Belfrey church and York Minster.

Further worries are caused by the way the forces supposedly threatening us frequently dissolve under deeper analysis. In particular, the notion of a unitary al-Qaeda proved as unsustainable on close inspection as did various of the early modern popish plots, and in particular the spectre of a unified and untiringly hostile Catholicism uniting the Pope, Spain and the Jesuits which was so potent in 1605. One thing which studying the history of Europe in the sixteenth and seventeenth centuries does is help understand how this type of mindset works. The British security services now seem convinced that the real threat from Islamic fundamentalists comes not from the much discussed al-Qaeda. Rather, it comes from loosely coordinated, indeterminate, 'bottom-up' organisations with varying degrees of autonomy. It is inevitable that such groupings should include a number of alienated young men: one can only hope that there is no Robert Catesby among them.

One is also struck by the parallels between the situation of English Catholics around 1605 and that of the generality of modern British Muslims, both of them groups of people attempting to maintain a religious and cultural identity in an environment which must at best seem vaguely antipathetic, and at worst is downright hostile. Whatever disadvantages they suffer or might feel they suffer, there is no formal or legal discrimination against British Muslims on a par with that which English Catholics once experienced. But the parallels are there, both for the Muslims and the wider society. Famously, in 1990 Norman Tebbit, a keen supporter of Mrs Thatcher and a man who had held high office under her, introduced supporting the English cricket team as a test for the degree to which immigrants had been assimilated into the English way of life. In the reign of Elizabeth I, Catholics under interrogation were asked the rather more fundamental question of how they would react if England were invaded by a foreign power trying to reintroduce Catholicism. The evidence we have suggests that the overwhelming majority of them would have stayed loyal.

The Fifth is finished as an anti-Catholic festival, and Guy Fawkes is burnt in effigy on a decreasing proportion of the nation's November bonfires. So what does the future hold for the Fifth? Obviously it will continue to be celebrated, unless government firework regulations and insurance premiums drive it out of existence. It will continue to be celebrated in various ways, and on a variety of levels: amongst families in back gardens, on a community level by villages or Parent Teacher Associations and the like, in the form of big firework displays with attendant funfairs run by local councils. And what the meaning of it is for those participating will, in the absence of sociological questionnaires, remain elusive. Ironically, we can probably reconstruct more of what celebrating the Fifth meant to a 5 November mob burning an effigy of the Pope in the 1670s or to a Lewes Bonfire Boy in the 1850s than we can for people watching a municipal firework display in modern Britain. Anthropologists have, from the inception of their discipline, made much of the analysis of rituals and ceremonies, and developed arguments about what these phenomena can lay bare about the deeper functionings of the societies where they occur, or even about the deeper mentalities of the individuals who inhabit those societies. Unfortunately, comparatively little of their research has been carried out on ritual in modern, complex societies. Perhaps, whatever its deeper significance, part of the reason why the Fifth has survived so long, and what would seem to guarantee its survival into the future, is that the British, as a people living in Northern Europe, need a festival to mark the beginning of winter, and that such a festival, as a challenge to the darkness and coldness to come, would best include bonfires and fireworks. Maybe Thomas Hardy was right when, in his musings on the fictional 5 November bonfires on Egdon Heath, he commented: 'to light a fire is the instinctive and resistant act of man when, at the winter ingress, the curfew is sounded throughout nature. It indicates a spontaneous, Promethean rebelliousness against the fiat that this recurrent season shall bring foul times, cold darkness, misery and death.'

The Fifth will continue, perhaps ever more circumscribed by fireworks regulations, police controls, fear for the nation's pets, and higher insurance premiums, perhaps increasingly achieving the status of an amorphous early winter fire festival, becoming conflated or running parallel with an ever more popular Hallowe'en. It has, after all, seen many changes in the past, and its history constitutes a remarkable story of continual reinvention. The very names it has been known under attest to this: Gunpowder Treason Day, Pope Day across the Atlantic, Guy Fawkes Night, Bonfire Night, Fireworks Night, each usage marking changes in how the Fifth might be envisaged. It has been celebrated as a deliverance from Catholicism, as a warning against treason, as an expression of fear of Catholic royal absolutism, as a demonstration against Catholic revival, as a cultural expression of rough plebeian customary festivities against the bourgeois respectability of the nineteenth-century town, as an occasion for upper-class hooliganism among Oxford undergraduates, as a municipal celebration, and as an opportunity for families to let off a few fireworks, gather together around a bonfire in their garden, and eat sausages and drink hot soup in defiance of the onset of winter. Unexpectedly and against the odds, the Fifth has survived for 400 years, constantly adapting as the times change, constantly taking on new meanings, standing in many ways as a symbol of broader changes in English and British life. And the survival of the Fifth has ensured that Guy Fawkes, again unexpectedly and against the odds, has remained one of the very few figures from England's past who enjoys an iconic status. He may be burnt progressively less frequently on Britain's November

bonfires, but the dour Yorkshire Catholic lives on in our consciousness, and in our affections. As long as this is the case,
memories of the events of 1605, however attenuated they
may become, will never quite be erased.

> Remember, remember, the Fifth of November,
> Gunpowder, Treason and Plot.
> I see no reason why Gunpowder Treason
> Should ever be forgot.

FURTHER READING

CHAPTER 1: THE EVIL EMPIRE AND THE ENEMY WITHIN

The description of the taking of Guy Fawkes comes from *The Gunpowder Plot: the Narrative of Oswald Tesimond alias Greenway*, trans. and ed. by Francis Edwards (London, 1973), which is one of the key Catholic sources for the history of the plot. Samuel Baker's notions of post-explosion destruction are found in his *A sermon preach'd at the Cathedral Church of York, November 5, 1745. Being the Anniversary thanksgiving, for our happy Deliverance from the most treacherous and bloody intended Massacre by Gunpowder* (York, 1745). For the Aberystwyth Centre for Explosion Studies estimates, see reports in the *Daily Telegraph*, 13 April 2003, and *Education Guardian*, 5 November 2003.

The best introduction to tales of Catholic atrocity is William S. Maltby, *The Black Legend in England: the Development of Anti-Spanish Sentiment, 1558–1600* (Durham, NC, 1971), while the St Bartholomew's Day massacres are described in Barbara B. Diefendorf, *Beneath the Cross: Catholics and Huguenots in sixteenth-century Paris* (Oxford, 1991). For an excellent analysis of English Protestant fears of Catholicism around 1600, see Carol Z. Wiener, 'The Beleaguered Isle: a Study of Elizabethan and Jacobean anti-Catholicism', *Past and Present*, 51 (1971).

There is an extensive literature on Catholicism in Elizabethan and early Stuart England. I have depended in particular on John Bossy, *The English Catholic Community 1570–1850* (London, 1975), and the more chronologically focused if less ambitious W.R. Trimble, *The Catholic Laity in Elizabethan England 1558–1603* (Cambridge, Mass., 1964). For specific aspects of the topic, see Hugh Aveling, *Northern Catholics: the Catholic Recusants of the North Riding of Yorkshire 1558–1790* (London, 1966), and Arnold Pritchard, *Catholic Loyalism in Elizabethan England* (London, 1979). John Bossy's quotation on Catholic women comes from his 'The Character of Elizabethan Catholicism', in Trevor Aston (ed.), *Crisis in Europe 1560–1660* (London, 1965). For a general discussion of women and recusancy, see Marie B. Rowlands, 'Recusant Women 1560–1640', in Mary Prior (ed.), *Women in English Society 1500–1800* (London and New York, 1985). K. Longley, *Saint Margaret Clitherow* (Wheathampsted, 1986), provides a good popular account of the Margaret Clitherow story.

Montague figures prominently in R.B. Manning, *Religion and Society in Elizabethan Sussex: a Study of the Enforcement of the Religious Settlement 1558–1603* (Leicester, 1969), while S. Kanshik, 'Resistance, Loyalty and Recusant Politics: Sir Thomas Tresham and the Elizabethan State', *Midland History*, 21 (1996), is an excellent study of Tresham's political position.

The classic work on Catesby is M. Whitmore Jones, *The Gunpowder Plot and the Life of Robert Catesby, also an Account of Chastleton House* (London, 1909). For a succinct recent account see the entry on Catesby by Mark Nicholls in *Oxford DNB*. I have also relied on Nicholls on the other Gunpowder plotters in *Oxford DNB*. Tesimond's views are found in *The Narrative of Oliver Tesimond alias Greenway*, and I have also

drawn on *Stuart Royal Proclamations*, ed. J.F. Larkin and Paul
L. Hughes (2 vols., Oxford, 1973). For a good recent discussion of Northumberland's importance, with special relevance to the events of 1605, see Mark Nicholls, *Investigating
Gunpowder Plot* (Manchester and New York, 1991), Part 2, 'The
Traitor? The Earl of Northumberland and the Gunpowder
Plot'. The classic study of Garnett remains Philip Caraman,
Henry Garnet 1555–1606 and the Gunpowder Plot (London,
1964). For Coke's opinions, see *A true and perfect Relation of
the Proceedings at the severall Arraignments of the late most barbarous Traitors* (London, 1606), an important contemporary
source.

CHAPTER 2: THE PLOT

There have been numerous histories of the Plot. My account is
based mainly on Mark Nicholls, *Investigating GunpowderPlot*
(Manchester and New York 1991), a scholarly work which
is especially strong on the governmental perspective on the
affair, and on a reliable popular history, Antonia Fraser, *The
Gunpowder Plot: Terror and Faith in 1605* (London, 1996). The
contemporary official history of the Gunpowder Plot was
laid out in *His Maiesties Speach in this last Session of Parliament,
as neere his very words as could be gathered at the Instant.
Together with a Discourse of the Maner of the Discovery of this
late intended Treason, ioyned with the Examination of some of the
Prisoners* (London, 1606). This should be read in conjunction
with two important histories of the plot written by contemporary Catholic observers: *The Gunpowder Plot: the Narrative
of Oswald Tesimond alias Greenway*, trans. and ed. Francis
Edwards (London, 1973), and *The Condition of Catholics under
James I: Father Gerard's Narrative of the Gunpowder Plot*, ed. J.S.

Morris (London, 1872). On the Mounteagle letter, see Henry Hawkes Spink, *The Gunpowder Plot and Lord Mounteagle's Letter: being a Proof, with moral Certitude, of the Authorship of the Document: together with some Account of the whole thirteen Gunpowder Conspirators* (London, 1902). Those with a taste for counterfactual history might enjoy reading Antonia Fraser, 'The Gunpowder Plot Succeeds', in Andrew Roberts (ed.), *What Might Have Been* (London, 2004).

Pauline Croft, *King James* (London, 2003), is an excellent, modern and balanced account of that much misunderstood monarch. For early modern views of James, see Robert Ashton (ed.), *James I by his Contemporaries* (London, 1969). Perhaps the most interesting work on James's religious beliefs is W.B. Patterson, *King James VI and I and the Reunion of Christendom* (Cambridge, 1997). Francis Bacon's comments come from J.R. Tanner, *Constitutional Documents of the Reign of King James I 1603–1625* (Cambridge, 1961), which contains most of the documents relevant to that aspect of the reign. The citations from James I's speech to Parliament come from a modern edition of his works, King James VI and I, *Political Writings*, ed. Johann P. Sommerville (Cambridge, 1994). I have also drawn on Godfrey Goodman, *The Court of King James the First* (2 vols., London, 1839). Salisbury awaits a good modern biography, but Pauline Croft, 'The Reputation of Robert Cecil: Libels, Political Opinion and Popular Awareness in the early Seventeenth Century', *Transactions of the Royal Historical Society*, 6th series, 1 (1991), is a good short introduction to his political importance. Nobody interested in English history can fail to read W.C. Sellar and R.J. Yeatman, *1066 and All That* (London, 1931, and numerous later editions).

For background to the Fawkes family, see Robert Davies,

The Fawkes's of York in the Sixteenth Century: including Notices of the early History of Guy Fawkes, the Gunpowder Plot Conspirator (London, 1850). Katherine M. Longley, 'Three Sites in the City of York', *Recusant History*, 12 (1973), contains an authoritative discussion of the location of the Fawkes family home. The army of Flanders is described in Geoffrey Parker, *The Army of Flanders and the Spanish Road 1567–1659: the Logistics of Spanish Victory and Defeat in the Low Countries' Wars* (Cambridge, 1972).

Garnett's involvement in the plot and his subsequent fate is discussed in Philip Caraman, *Henry Garnet 1555–1606 and the Gunpowder Plot* (London, 1964).

CHAPTER 3: REMEMBERING THROUGH THE SEVENTEENTH CENTURY

The key text on the trials is *A true and perfect Relation of the Proceedings at the severall Arraignments of the late most barbarous Traitors* (London, 1606). I have also drawn on the general histories of the Gunpowder Plot referred to above, and for Garnett's sufferings on Philip Caraman, *Henry Garnet 1555–1606 and the Gunpowder Plot* (London, 1964). For Montagu, see the entry in the *Oxford DNB*.

Contemporary official reactions are discussed by A.W.R.E. Okines, 'Why Was There So Little Reaction to Gunpowder Plot?', *Journal of Ecclesiastical History*, 55 (2004). Quotations from William Barlow and James I come from William Barlow, *The Sermon Preached at Paules Crosse, the tenth Day of November, being the Sunday after the Discoverie of this late horrible Treason* (London, 1606), and James VI and I, *Political Writings*, ed. Johann P. Sommerville (Cambridge, 1994).

The early history of the commemoration of the Fifth

is described in David Cressy, *Bonfires and Bells: National Memory and the Protestant Calendar in Elizabethan and Stuart England* (London, 1989); Ronald Hutton, *The Rise and Fall of Merry England: the Ritual Year 1400–1700* (Oxford, 1994), and Ronald Hutton, *The Stations of the Sun: a History of the Ritual Year in Britain* (Oxford, 1996), which also contains a useful discussion of All Saints' and All Souls' Days. The incident in Dorchester is noted in David Underdown, *Fire from Heaven: Life in an English Town in the Seventeenth Century* (London, 1992). On providence, see Alexandra Walsham, *Providence in Early Modern England* (Oxford, 1997), which contains an excellent discussion of how commemoration of the Fifth was adjusted to this ideological template.

Contemporary sources drawn on include: Thomas Taylor, *A Mappe of Rome: lively exhibiting her mercilesse Meeknesse, and cruell Mercies to the Church of God: preached in five Sermons, on Occasion of the Gunpowder Treason* (London, 1619); Cornelius Burges, *Another Sermon preached to the Honorable House of Commons now assembled in Parliament, November the Fifth, 1641* (London, 1641); *The Diary of Samuel Pepys*, ed. Robert Latham and William Matthews (11 vols., London, 1970–83); *The Diary of Ralph Josselin, 1616–1683*, ed. Alan Macfarlane (Records of Economic and Social History, new series, 3, 1976); *The Burning of the Whore of Babylon, as it was acted, with great Applause, in the Poultrey, London, on Wednesday night (being the 5th of November) at Six of the Clock* (London, 1673); Narcissus Luttrell, *A Brief Historical Relation of State Affairs from September 1678 to April 1714* (6 vols., Oxford, 1857); *Calendar of State Papers Domestic 1682*; *The Diary of John Evelyn*, ed. E.S. de Beer (6 vols., Oxford, Oxford University Press, 1955), Gilbert Burnet, *A Sermon preached before the House of Peers in the Abbey of Westminster on the 5th of November 1689. Being Gun-Powder*

Treason Day, as likewise the Day of his Majesties Landing in England (London, 1689). Although I have not mentioned it in the text, readers might also be interested in the existence of a doggerel tract which, unusually, mentions Guy Fawkes, the anonymous *Faux's Ghost: or, Advice to Papists* (London, 1680).

There is an extensive literature on the history of the popish Plot and the Exclusion Crisis. The general reader would gain much from two classic studies, J.P. Kenyon, *The Popish Plot* (London, 1972), and J.R. Jones, *The First Whigs: The Politics of the Exclusion Crisis* (Oxford, 1961). On the popular dimension of the politics of the period, see Tim Harris, *London Crowds in the Reign of Charles II: Propaganda and Politics from the Restoration until the Exclusion Crisis* (Cambridge, 1987), while one of the more celebrated incidents of the period is analysed by Alan Marshal, *The Strange Death of Edmund Godfrey: Plots and Politics in Restoration London* (Stroud, 1999). O.W. Furley, 'The Pope Burning Processions of the Late Seventeenth Century', *History*, 44 (1959), is very relevant to our story.

CHAPTER 4: CHANGING TIMES AND THE REINVENTION OF GUY FAWKES

Amyot's views on the Fifth are contained in *Youth and Revolution in the 1790s: Letters of William Pattisson, Thomas Amyot and Henry Crabb Robinson*, ed. Penelope J. Corfield and Chris Evans (Stroud, 1996).

On the Sacheverell Affair, see Geoffrey Holmes, *The Trial of Dr Sacheverell* (London, 1973). Sacheverell's sermon was entitled *The Perils of false Brethren, both in Church, and State: set forth in a Sermon preach'd before the Right Honourable the Lord*

Mayor, Aldermen and Citizens of London; at the Cathedral-Church of St Paul, on the 5th of November, 1709 (London, 1709).

The sermons referred to include: *The Whole Works of that most reverend Father in God, Sir William Dawes, Brt, Late Archbishop of York, Primate of England and Metropolitan* (3 vols., London, 1733); Philip Stubs, *The Church of England under God, an impregnable Bulwark against Popery* (London, 1704); John Garnett, *A Sermon preached in Christ Church, Dublin, on Monday, the 5th of November 1753, being the Anniversary of the Gunpowder-Plot and of the happy Arrival of King William III* (Dublin, 1753).

For the fortunes of England's Roman Catholic community over the eighteenth and early nineteenth centuries, see John Bossy, *The English Catholic Community 1570–1850* (London, 1975), and Michael Mullett, *Catholics in Britain and Ireland, 1558–1829* (Basingstoke, 1998). Owen Chadwick, *The Victorian Church* (2 vols., London, 1966) provides a useful background to the religious developments of the period.

For the dramatic works cited, see: www.bcpl.net/ ~hutmanpr/fawkestheater.html, *Guy Fawkes or the Fifth of November: a Prelude in One Act*; www.bcpl.net/~/cbladey/ guy/html/panto.html, *Harlequin and Guy Fawkes: Or, the Fifth of November: a Comic Pantomime*, p. 5. www.bcpl. net~hutmanpr/andspoons.html, *Guy Fawkes: the Ugly Mug and the Couple of Spoons*; www.bcpl.net/~hutmanpr/king-match2.html, *Guy Fawkes or a Match for a King II*; and www. bcpl.net/~hutmanpr/kingmatch.html, *Guy Fawkes, or a Match for a King*, p. 41; Edward Stirling, *Guido Fawkes: or, the Prophetess of Ordsall Cave: a Melo Drama* (Duncombe's edn, London, n.d.); and George Macfarren, *Guy Faux: or, the Gunpowder Treason: an Historical Melo-Drama in Three Acts* (Cumberland's Minor Theatre edn, London, 1879).

William Harrison Ainsworth, *Guy Fawkes, or the Gunpowder Treason: an Historical Romance* (3 vols., London, 1841) is an admirable guide to how the image of Fawkes and the plot were changing. On Ainsworth, see S.M. Ellis, *William Harrison Ainsworth and his Friends* (2 vols., London, 1911), and Stephen James Carver, *The Life and Works of the Lancashire Novelist William Harrison Ainsworth* (Lewiston etc., 2003). Both these works contain discussions of Ainsworth's novel on the Gunpowder Plot. For a typical example of later popular works on Fawkes and the Plot, see *The Boyhood Days of Guy Fawkes: or, the Conspirators of Old London* (London, ?1905).

The historical works referred to (giving the editions cited) are: David Jardine, *A Narrative of the Gunpowder Plot* (London, 1857); John Lingard, *The History of England from the Invasion by the Romans to the Accession of William and Mary in 1668* (10 vols., Dublin, 1874); J.R. Green, *A Short History of the English People* (4 vols., London, 1892–4); S.R. Gardiner, *The History of England from the Accession of James I to the Outbreak of the Civil War 1603–1642* (10 vols., London, 1905 edn); Winston S. Churchill, *A History of the English Speaking Peoples* (4 vols., London, 1956); John Gerard, *What was the Gunpowder Plot? The Traditional Story Tested by Original Evidence* (London, 1897); S.R. Gardiner, *What Gunpowder Plot Was* (London, 1987); Francis Edwards, *Guy Fawkes: the Real Story of the Gunpowder Plot?* (London, 1969); and G.M. Trevelyan, *History of England* (2nd impression, London, 1926). For an informative and entertaining discussion of many of these historians, see John Kenyon, *The History Men: the Historical Profession in England since the Renaissance* (London, 1983). The eighteenth-century tract which revived the Salisbury involvement theory was the anonymous *An Essay towards a new History of the Gun-Powder Treason, wherein its real Origine, Cause and Design, are candidly set forth* (London, 1765).

The sermons referred to in the later section of this chapter include: Ralph Churton, *The Reality of the Powder Plot vindicated from some recent Misrepresentations. A Sermon preached before the University of Oxford at St Mary's; on Tuesday, Nov 5, 1805* (Oxford, 1806); Edward Bickersteth, *The Divine warning to the Church, at this Time, of our present Enemies, Dangers, and Duties, and as to our future Prospects* (London, 1842); Robert J. M'Ghee, *A Sermon Preached at Harold's Cross Church, Dublin, on Sunday, November 5, 1843* (Dublin, 1843); Joseph Oldknow, *A sermon preached in the Holy Trinity Chapel, Bordesley, Birmingham, on the Morning of the twenty-first Sunday after Trinity, 1843, being the Anniversary of the Gunpowder Treason* (London, 1843). Reading the entries on Churton and Bickersteth in the *Oxford DNB* helps contextualise their 5 November sermons.

CHAPTER 5: THE TRIUMPH AND TAMING OF BONFIRE NIGHT

William Hone, *The Every-Day and Table Book; or, an everlasting Calendar of popular Amusements, Sports, Pastimes, Ceremonies, Manners, Customs and Events* (3 vols., London, 1838), contains a lengthy discussion of the 5 November celebrations of its day. The description of the 1715 celebration comes from Julien Hoppit, *A Land of Liberty? England 1689–1727* (Oxford, 2000), while the full title of the farce against Thomas Bradbury is *Make a Noise Tom, A Farce. Occasioned by the Lighting of a Loyal Bonfire with that Brush of Iniquity Mr B___y, who was burnt in Effigie in the Town of Wakefield in Yorkshire* (London, 1718).

For Pope Day and celebrations of the Fifth in colonial

America more generally, see: David Cressy, *Bonfires and Bells: National Memory and the Protestant Calendar in Elizabethan and Stuart England* (London, 1989), Simon P. Newman, *Parades and the Politics of the Street: Festive Culture in the Early American Republic* (Philadelphia, 1997); Peter Shaw, *American Patriots and the Rituals of Revolution* (Cambridge, Mass., 1981).

For excellent introductions to the fortunes of the Fifth in nineteenth-century England, see Robert D. Storch, '"Please to Remember the Fifth of November": Conflict, Solidarity and Public Order in Southern England, 1815–1900', in Robert D. Storch (ed.), *Popular Culture in Nineteenth-century England* (London, 1982), and David Cressy, 'The Fifth of November Remembered', in Roy Porter (ed.), *Myths of the English* (Cambridge, 1992). I have based my account of the Fifth at Lewes on James Edward Etherington, 'The Sociology of a Recurrent Ceremonial Drama: Lewes Guy Fawkes Night, 1800–1913' (PhD dissertation, Open University, 1988), and Etherington, *Lewes Bonfire Night: a Short History of the Guy Fawkes Celebrations* (S.B. Publications, Seaford, East Sussex, 1993), which is an excellent and well-illustrated popular account. For an important discussion of the complex religious background in the town, see Jeremy Goring, *Burn Holy Fire; Religion in Lewes Since the Reformation* (Cambridge, 2003). For Guildford, see Gavin Morgan, *The Guildford Guy Riots: Being an Exact Description of the Terrible Disturbances in the County Town of Surrey* (Guildford, 1992). For Exeter, see Roger Swift, 'Guy Fawkes celebrations in Exeter', *History Today*, 31 (November 1981), and Robert Newton, *Victorian Exeter* (Leicester, 1968). For Northamptonshire, D.G. Paz, 'Bonfire Night in Mid Victorian Northamptonshire: the Politics of a Popular Revel', *Historical Research*, 63 (1990), which is of special interest in demonstrating how future research might

unearth local variations on the theme of Bonfire Night celebrations in Victorian England. The description of the Malton
riot comes from *The Times*, 7 November 1867. The attack on
Isaac White was reported in *The Times*, 11 November 1862.

Apart from references given in the text, this account of
Oxford undergraduate celebrations is based on reports
in *Jackson's Oxford Journal*, 10 November 1906; *Jackson's
Oxford Journal*, 9 November 1907; *Oxford Mail*, 5 November
1932; *Oxford Mail*, 6 November 1929. For background, see
*The History of Oxford University, Vol. 7, Nineteenth-Century
Oxford, Part 2*, ed. M.G. Brock and M.C. Curthoys (Oxford,
2000), which also contains further details of 5 November
incidents.

Comprehensive details on printed works dealing with
fireworks are provided by Chris Philip, *A Bibliography of
Fireworks Books: Works on Recreative Fireworks from the Sixteenth
to the Twentieth Century* (Winchester, 1985). For nineteenth-
century developments, see Alan St H. Brock, *A History of
Fireworks* (London, 1949), and www.blackcatfireworks.
ltd.uk?company/?page=history2, 'History of Standard
Fireworks'. The story of the British firework industry is
brought up to date by www.cyber-heritage.co.uk/industry/,
'A look at the Orientalisation of the British Firework Industry
in the 1990s'. Other than those referenced in the text, the accidents described are reported in *The Times*, 29 October 1856 and
14 October 1868.

CHAPTER 6: WINTER FIRES

Those interested in the present-day celebrations at Lewes
should visit the Lewes Bonfire Council's Homepage, www.
lewesbonfirecouncil.org.uk, which refers visitors to the

individual Lewes Societies' websites. Further details for 5 November 2004 in Lewes come from www.bbc.co.uk/dna/collective/A863408. Other society websites consulted were: www.edenbridgetown.com/bonfire/index_night/bonfire_society/index.shtml and www.freewebs.com.bonfire/index1.htm/, The Battel Bonfire Boyes Official Website.

Description of events in 2004 are based on numerous websites and newspapers of the time, notably: Icwales. icnetwork.co.uk/0900entertainment/0050artsnews/tm-objectid=1483395; www.manchesteronline.co.uk/news/s/136/136026; *News and Star*, 8 November 2004; *Evening News*, 8 November 2004; *Express and Star*, 6 November 2004; *Liverpool Echo*, 26 October 2004; *Manchester Evening News*, 2 November 2004; *Evening Mail*, 26 October 2004; www.ukpets.co.uk/ukp/archive/news_items1_814php; www.wildlifetrusts.org/index.php?section=news&id=909.

ThediscussionofthecurrentfortunesoftheFifthanditsprospects for the future draws on Thomas Hardy, *The Return of the Native* (Penguin Classics edn, Harmondsworth, 1999); David Cressy, *Bonfires and Bells: National Memory and the Protestant Calendar in Elizabethan and Stuart England* (London, 1989); Ronald Hutton, *The Stations of the Sun: a History of the Ritual Year in Britain* (Oxford, 1996); www.tarbarrels.co.uk/main.asp; www.britannia.com.history/devon/otbarrel.html; Stephen Hayward, 'HalloweenSpreebeatsGuyFawkes', *SundayMirror*, 17 October 2004; and Daniel J. Crowley, 'Guy Fawkes Day and Fresh Creek, Andros Island', *Man*, 58 (1958). Hutton's *Stations of the Sun* is particularly recommended as a work in which an academichistoriancastsawell-informed,shrewd,scepticalbut sympatheticeyeoverpopularcustomsandpopularbeliefs.

On the 'End of History' see Francis Fukuyama, *The End of History and the Last Man* (Harmondsworth, 1992).

LIST OF ILLUSTRATIONS

1. Illustration by George Cruikshank for William Harrison Ainsworth, *Guy Fawkes, or the Gunpowder Treason: an Historical Romance* (3 vols., London, 1841): University of York Library.
2. Illustration from John Foxe, *Actes and Monuments of Matters most speciall and memorable, happening in the Church, with a universall Historie of the same* (Religious Tract Society edition, 8 vols., London, 1877): University of York Library.
3. Illustration from an early edition of Richard Verstegan, *Theatrum Crudelitatis Haereticorum nostri Temporis*: Author's Collection.
4. The frontispiece to *The Workes of that most high and mightie Prince, James: by the Grace of God, King of Great Britaine, France and Ireland, defender of the Faith, &c* (London, 1616): University of York Library.
5. Section of the parish register of St Michael-le-Belfrey, York: © Reproduced by kind permission of the Dean and Chapter of York.
6. Detail from *Portraits of the Gunpowder Plotters, and Representations of their Punishments,* a print of 1606: University of York Library.

7. Illustration from Francis Herring, *Mischeefes Mysterie: or, Treasons Master-peece* (London, 1617): © The Dean and Chapter of York: by kind permission.

8. An illustration by George Cruikshank for Ainsworth's *Guy Fawkes, or the Gunpowder Treason*: University of York Library.

9. A detail from Samuel Ward, *To God, in Memorye of his Double Deliverance from the Invincible Navie and the Unmatchable Powder Treason* (Amsterdam, 1621). © The Dean and Chapter of York: by kind permission.

10. Reproduction of seventeenth-century print from J.R. Green, *A Short History of the English People* (4 Vols., London, 1892–4): University of York Library.

11. Detail from *Portraits of the Gunpowder Plotters, and Representations of their Punishments*, a print of 1606: BMC 71: Courtesy of the Trustees of the British Museum, with additional thanks to ProQuest. This illustration originally appeared in the British Satirical Prints Series, published by Chadwyck Healey in 1986.

12. Illustration by George Cruikshank for Ainsworth's *Guy Fawkes, or the Gunpowder Treason*: University of York Library.

13. The title page of *His Maiesties Speach in this last Session of Parliament* (London, 1606): © The Dean and Chapter of York: by kind permission.

14. The title page to John Williams, *The History of the Powder-Treason* (London, 1680); © The Dean and Chapter of York: by kind permission.

15. The title page of Gilbert Burnet, *A Sermon preached before the House of Peers in the Abbey of Westminster, on the 5th of November 1689* (London, 1689): © The Dean and Chapter of York: by kind permission.

16. From James Gillray, *The Works of James Gillray from the original Plates: with the addition of many Subjects not before collected* (2 vols., London, 1851): University of York Library.
17. *A Genuine Dandy or a Walking Guy*, print of 1818 by Marks, BMC 13083: Courtesy of the Trustees of the British Museum, with additional thanks to ProQuest. This illustration originally appeared in the British Satirical Prints Series, published by Chadwyck Healey in 1986.
18. Illustration by George Cruikshank for Ainsworth's *Guy Fawkes, or the Gunpowder Treason*: University of York Library.
19. Illustration by George Cruikshank for William Hone, *The Every-day and Table Book; or, Everlasting Calendar of Popular Amusements, Sports, Pastimes, Ceremonies, Manners, Customs and Events* (3 vols., London, 1838): University of York Library.
20. *Punch*, November 1850: University of York Library.
21. A handbill of 1850: Author's Collection.
22. *Punch*, November 1849: University of York Library.
23. From A.R. Wright, *British Calendar Customs: England, vol. III, Fixed Festivals, June–December Inclusive* (London, 1940): Photograph: The Folklore Society, London.
24. Photograph © Peter Varnham: by kind permission.
25. Photograph © Peter Varnham: by kind permission.
26. Photograph © St Mary's Music School, Edinburgh: by kind permission.
27. Photograph © James Sharpe.
28. Photograph © James Sharpe.

ACKNOWLEDGEMENTS

The idea for writing this book originated in a coffee-break conversation with a colleague, Bill Sheils. We had just given some public lectures to commemorate the 400th anniversary of the death of Elizabeth I, and Bill opined that we would probably find ourselves similarly occupied in November 2005, with the 400th anniversary of the Gunpowder Plot. I mused on the possibility of writing a book on how celebrations on 5 November had changed over the four centuries after 1605, this being an issue which had been of sporadic interest to me for some time. On the way home in the car that night, I mentioned my idea for a book to my wife, but voiced my doubts about being able to complete such a work to a tight schedule: she replied forcefully, in terms that I shall not repeat here, that she was confident that, in my position, she could. In the event, we both found ourselves in that nightmare situation for a couple of married academics, both trying to complete books at the same time. But I am grateful for her stiffening my resolve initially, and for her subsequent support. Thanks for support must also be extended to my agent, Jane Turnbull, and to Andrew Franklin at Profile.

Other support came from institutions: the British Library, the J.B. Morrell Library of the University of York, the Borthwick Institute for Archives, York Minster Library, York

Minster Archives, and the Centre for Oxfordshire Studies. I am especially grateful to the staff of the photography department in the J.B. Morrell Library for the speed and efficiency with which they met my requests for help with most of the illustrations in this book.

INDEX